Course 2001:
Instructional Guide

ASL Grammatical Aspects:
Comparative Translations

Authors:
Jenna Cassell & Eileen McCaffrey

©1995 Sign Enhancers, Inc. All Rights Reserved.

Acknowledgments

A heartfelt thank you to: Greg, Claire and Geoffrey McCaffrey for creating such a peaceful and loving space amidst the giant madrones in which this book just flowed, Kelley Forseth for sharing a form in which to put our ideas, Shelly Gourlay who put hours of dedicated nit-picking (should nit-picking be hyphenated?) into the manuscript, Dan Meireis at L. Grafix for his technical prowess and generous nature, Jane Lucas at Lynx for her unending support and shared knowledge of publishing, Angela Willis at Logistics for turning the whole project into a physical reality and to Sara Sullivan, the CMP coordinator at the Registry of Interpreters for the Deaf, for her enthusiastic support of reaching more interpreters through creative independent study options.

Last, but definately not least, we sincerely thank the talent on the video and CD-ROM, Billy Seago, Jenna Cassell, Nathie Marbury and Jack R. Cassell. Their willingness to share their talent assists greatly in maintaining the linguistic integrity of the language learned by those who take this course.

This Instructional Guide is a co-creation that now, as a seed planted in soil, takes root to spread new possibilities of skill development to interpreters.

Proudly produced and published by:

Sign Enhancers, Inc.
1535 State St.
Salem, OR 97301
1-800-767-4461 (v/tty)

Course 2001 Introduction

The authors of <u>ASL Grammatical Aspects: Comparative Translations</u> were interested in providing an innovative response to several long-standing needs in the fields of Sign Language interpretation and ASL instruction. This first-of-its-kind course offers 20 hours of linguistic and skill development activities in response to the following needs:

User-friendly Instructional Resource

Instructional resources in the form of a user-friendly, effective curriculum with corresponding instructional media available to educators of advanced ASL and interpretation have been virtually non-existent. Educators who have wanted such materials have had to create it themselves. The course, including this Instructional Guide, Videotape and CD-ROM, includes everything necessary for offering a complete 20 hour course.

Empowering Students: Self-Directed Skill Development

In response to the lack of opportunities for advanced skill development for students of both ASL and interpretation, the authors were interested in creating a mechanism by which these individuals could be empowered to enhance their own skills. The step by step instructions allow learners to take this course as an independent study. The methodologies used can be applied over and over for long-term, self-directed skill development.

Comparative Translations: ASL, English & PSE

Another need addressed by this course is to help resolve issues around the difference between ASL, English and Pidgin Sign English (PSE), also referred to as "Contact Signing." Since PSE is <u>not</u> a language, but a combination of elements from both ASL and English, there has been much confusion around how to define it. This course, with the companion instructional media (videotape and CD-ROM) assists learners in seeing a comparison between ASL, written English and PSE. Specific grammatical aspects are explained, followed by demonstrations of how these ASL grammatical aspects can be incorporated within PSE to maximize the clarity of such communications. A unique visual comparison is provided in the context of manageable sentences in order to assist learners to better respond to the preferences of consumers requesting the use of PSE as applied to transliteration services.

Table of Contents

Course Overview
Course Goals 1
Course Components 2
Educator Preparation 6
Independent Study Option 7
Translation Glossing System 9
Overview Summary 10

Getting Started
A.1   Course Objectives 11
A.2   Pretest: Written Portion 12
A.3   Pretest: Performance Portion 16
A.4   Mini-Lecture: ASL 17
A.5   Linguistic Information: ASL 18
A.6   Mini-Lecture: PSE 19
A.7   Linguistic Information: PSE 20

Module 1: Topic/Comment Structure
1.1   Mini-Lecture 21
1.2   Linguistic Information 22
1.3   Instructional Activity 24
1.4   Video Practice Activity 26
1.5   Module Review 27
1.6   Skills Application 30

Module 2: Yes/No Questions
2.1   Mini-Lecture 31
2.2   Linguistic Information 32
2.3   Instructional Activity 33
2.4   Video Practice Activity 34
2.5   Instructional Activity 35
2.6   Instructional Activity 36
2.7   Module Review 37
2.8   Skills Application 39

Module 3: Wh-Questions
3.1   Mini-Lecture 40
3.2   Linguistic Information 40
3.3   Instructional Activity 41
3.4   Video Practice Activity 43
3.5   Module Review 44
3.6   Skills Application 47

Module 4: Rhetorical Questions
4.1   Mini-Lecture 48
4.2   Linguistic Information 49
4.3   Video Practice Activity 50
4.4   Instructional Activity 51
4.5   Module Review 52
4.6   Skills Application 55

Module 5: Directionality
5.1 Mini-Lecture 56
5.2 Linguistic Information 57
5.3 Instructional Activity 58
5.4 Video Practice Activity 59
5.5 Instructional Activity 60
5.6 Module Review 61
5.7 Skills Application 63

Module 6: Use of Space
6.1 Mini-Lecture 64
6.2 Linguistic Information 65
6.3 Video Practice Activity 66
6.4 Instructional Activity 67
6.5 Module Review 68
6.6 Skills Application 71

Module 7: Negation
7.1 Mini-Lecture 72
7.2 Linguistic Information 73
7.3 Video Practice Activity 74
7.4 Instructional Activity 75
7.5 Module Review 76
7.6 Skills Application 78

Module 8: Classifiers
8.1 Mini-Lecture 79
8.2 Linguistic Information 80
8.3 Instructional Activity 81
8.4 Video Practice Activity 82
8.5 Instructional Activity 83
8.6 Module Review 84
8.7 Skills Application 86

Module 9: Conditionals
9.1 Mini-Lecture 87
9.2 Linguistic Information 88
9.3 Instructional Activity 89
9.4 Video Practice Activity 90
9.5 Module Review 91
9.6 Skills Application 93

Module 10: Time Sequenced Ordering
10.1 Mini-Lecture 94
10.2 Linguistic Information 95
10.3 Video Practice Activity 96
10.4 Instructional Activity 97
10.5 Module Review 98
10.6 Skills Application 99

Assessment
Assessment: Written Portion 101
Assessment: Performance Portion 105

Appendix
Answer Keys 107
Additional Resources 109

COURSE GOALS

The authors' primary concerns in creating this course were to provide a curriculum capable of enhancing formal interpreter education, offering professional development and certification maintenance, preparing individuals for certification, and introducing grammatical aspects to students of ASL.

Enhancing Formal Interpreter Education

The standardization of instruction within interpreter education has long been a goal of educators throughout the US and Canada. This Instructional Guide provides an avenue for standardizing content and a methodology for enhancing the overall quality of interpreter education. Beyond the scope of a textbook, this instructional package provides all the curriculum components needed to offer the course including: objectives, linguistic content, step-by-step skill development exercises, instructional media, and assessment tools.

The first goal of this course is to complement existing interpreter education curricula in formal programs throughout the US and Canada, facilitating its use by educators in those programs. Interpreter educators may incorporate these course materials into current course work to enhance the effectiveness of the educational opportunities presented to their students. Depending on student skill levels, interpreter educators are encouraged to make appropriate modifications in the delivery of this course, and to provide additional support and feedback to their students.

Offering Professional Development
and Certification Maintenance for Interpreters

The second goal of this course is to answer the need for on-going professional development and certification maintenance for certified interpreters. Traditionally, access to skill and knowledge enhancement was dependent on infrequent and expensive workshops and seminars. Too few and far between, these have been inadequate to meet the needs of working interpreters who wish to enhance their professional abilities.

This course offers certified interpreters a non-traditional approach to professional development and certification maintenance. In fact, this carefully designed course allows professional interpreters to utilize independent study as an option of the Certification Maintenance Program (CMP) offered by the Registry of Interpreters for the Deaf (RID). When registered with an RID-approved sponsor, an individual may earn up to 2.0 Continuing Education Units (CEU) credits from RID to be applied toward certification maintenance. For more information on how to obtain credits for this course, see the "Independent Study Option" section in this Guide.

Instructional Guide
©1995 Sign Enhancers, Inc.

Course 2001: Course Overview

Preparing Individuals for Certification

A third goal of this course is to provide professional development opportunities to working interpreters who aspire to achieve certification. This Instructional Guide can serve as a working guide for skill development, leading to increasing the quality and quantity of certified interpreters.

Introducing ASL Grammatical Aspects

A final goal of this course is to provide individuals with information regarding grammatical aspects of ASL. Advanced students of ASL may take this course independently, or this Instructional Guide can serve to supplement ASL coursework within an existing program.

COURSE COMPONENTS

Detailed descriptions of all instructional components are provided for the educator or independent study learner. The instructor or learner should take note of all required items, and ensure that these items are obtained prior to beginning the course. All materials have been produced by and are available through Sign Enhancers, Inc.

Required Instructional Media

The content of this curriculum is demonstrated and supported by the videotape entitled *Grammar & Sentence Structures* and the CD-ROM entitled *Vocabulary, Grammar & Sentences*. Therefore, at least one of these items is a required companion to this Instructional Guide. For interpreter education programs utilizing this course, it is recommended that the videotape be used for in-class sessions and the CD-ROM for individual home/lab work. If a computer is not available, each student should have a personal copy of the videotape, or the videotape should be available in a lab setting. For individuals taking the course for independent study, either the CD-ROM or the videotape would be a required companion to this guide.

Descriptions of required companion instructional media follow.

Videotape

This course is based upon the samples provided in the instructional videotape entitled *Grammar & Sentence Structures.* It provides linguistic information regarding the following ten grammatical topic areas:

1. Topic/Comment Structure
2. Yes/No Question Formats
3. Wh-Question Formats
4. Rhetorical Question Formats
5. Directionality
6. Use of Space
7. Negation
8. Classifiers
9. Conditionals
10. Time Sequenced Ordering

The information is introduced in mini-lectures (presented in ASL) by nationally-known ASL instructor, Nathie Marbury. Each mini-lecture is skillfully voice interpreted by RID certified interpreter, Bonnie Sherwood. Closed captioning is also provided for these segments.

Each mini-lecture focuses on a specific grammatical topic area. The linguistic information is reinforced with sample sentences clearly demonstrating each grammatical feature. The sentences are presented by celebrated signing models Billy Seago, Jenna Cassell, Nathie Marbury and Jack R. Cassell.

Instructional Guide
©1995 *Sign Enhancers, Inc.*

Each modeled sample includes:

1. The written English sentence shown on the screen.
2. A signed rendition of the sentence using PSE.
3. An interpretation of the sentence using ASL.

This unique videotape allows the learner to practice transliteration and interpretation skills with manageable chunks of information presented in sentences. A valuable comparison of PSE and ASL can easily be noted.

The videotape length is 60 minutes, providing ample examples of each grammatical topic area and a motherlode of practice material for skill development.

CD-ROM

The same instructional material is available on the CD-ROM entitled, *Vocabulary, Grammar & Sentences*. Because of the non-linear format, the CD-ROM allows learners ready access to the sample sentences. The mini-lectures are replaced with more extensive text files, including an audio version option. There are several additional features provided in the CD-ROM not available on the videotape, such as interactive games and tests, audio clips, and speed control of the videotape samples.

The CD-ROM runs on a PC with Windows 3.1 or higher.

Instructional Guide

This Instructional Guide provides learners with a comprehensive step-by-step plan including: objectives, a pretest, ten instructional modules, and an assessment. The user-friendly instructions maximize learning outcomes.

The following elements are included:

Pretest

The pretest is to be taken prior to starting the course, and consists of both written and performance portions.

a) Pretest: Written Portion

The written portion of the pretest consists of 25 true/false, multiple choice, and check-list questions. The written pretest covers the linguistic information included in the course. The results of this pretest should be retained to allow comparison of the learner's knowledge prior to and following completion of this course.

Note: An answer key is provided in the Appendix. To maximize the instructional benefit of this process, do <u>not</u> refer to this key until after the final assessment has been completed and submitted.

b) Pretest: Performance Portion

The performance portion of the pretest provides ten sentences (interpreters are to record these sentences onto an audio tape to simulate the interpreting task) to be signed using PSE and signed again using ASL. This pretest is a means of assessing the learner's current skill level.

For the ASL segment, instructions specify which grammatical features are to be applied to each sample. The learner's performance should be videotaped to allow a comparison between skills prior to and following completion of this course.

Module Layout

The format of the instructional modules have been carefully designed to maximize ease-of-use by the instructor and learner. Following are complete descriptions of each element of the format. The information is arranged in two columns with easy-to-read headings on the left, and course content on the right, as demonstrated below:

LEFT COLUMN	RIGHT COLUMN
Module # **Topic Area**	There are ten modules in this course. Each module is clearly identified with a number and the topic area to be covered. Each module includes: 1. Mini-Lecture 2. Linguistic Information 3. Instructional Activities a) Activity Goals b) Activity Instructions c) Learning Tips d) Time Allotment 4. Module Review 5. Skills Application Exercise
Mini-Lecture	Each module includes viewing a mini-lecture presented on the videotape in ASL by Nathie Marbury, with voice interpretations skillfully provided by RID-certified interpreter, Bonnie Sherwood. Learners are given the opportunity to view these lectures (without voice) and to create a summary of the content presented. This activity enhances understanding of the underlying grammatical aspects of each module. Learners may check their answers by listening to the model-voiced interpretations or take advantage of the closed captions provided for these videotape segments.

Linguistic Information The grammatical aspects of the topic area presented in each module are further delineated in this section. Linguistic explanations support learners as they apply this information to the instructional activities throughout the module.

Instructional Activities

Activity Title Activities are identified with a title. The title includes a fun hint regarding the focus of each particular activity.

Activities are assigned a number. The first number identifies the module in which the activity occurs, and the second number indicates the sequence in which the activity takes place within the module.

Time Allotted An estimate of the minimum amount of time required for each activity is provided. If learners wish to spend more time reviewing an activity, they should be encouraged to do so.

Activity Goal All activities have a clearly expressed goal. This allows learners to develop appropriate expectations regarding possible learning outcomes.

Activity Instructions Step-by-step instructions are given for each activity. Action words are used for clarity. These words, such as **VIEW, PRACTICE, PLAY TAPE, STOP TAPE**, appear in capital letters and boldface type. They signal an action for the instructor/learner to take.

 A video icon indicates activities requiring use of the companion videotape/CD-ROM.

Learning Tip *In italics, these helpful tips are shared to supplement the module activities.*

Module Review   Instructional modules include a review of all the material presented, including an opportunity to practice applying the grammatical feature to sample sentences.

A written script of the samples demonstrates each sentence three ways:
       a) Written English sentence.
       b) Gloss for PSE rendition.
       c) Gloss for ASL rendition.

Skills Application   Instructional modules close with an opportunity for learners to practice applying the grammatical feature addressed in the module to new practice sentences.

Assessment

This Instructional Guide includes an assessment tool with which learners assess knowledge and skill levels following the course. The Assessments include the following portions:

a) Assessment: Written Portion

The written portion of the assessment consists of 25 true/false, multiple choice, and check-list questions. These questions reference linguistic information covered in the course. A comparison can be made with the learner's pretest results.

b) Assessment: Performance Portion

The performance portion of the assessment provides 20 sentences (interpreters are to record these sentences onto an audio tape to simulate the interpreting task) to be signed using PSE and signed again using ASL. This assessment is a means of determining post-course skill level.

For the ASL segment, instructions specify which grammatical features are to be applied to each sample. The learner's performance should be videotaped to allow a comparison between skills prior to and following completion of this course.

EDUCATOR PREPARATION

For instructors using this course in a classroom setting, the following list provides a detailed, step-by-step preparation guide for offering this course:

1. Read this guide and review entire curriculum.

2. Assess how this course fits into your current course offering.

3. Make selections of activities and plan the overall scheduling of activities to customize the course to fit your students' needs.

4. To enhance instruction, consider which of your own personal experiences, skills, knowledge or other resources you wish to share with students.

5. Confirm you have ordered and received your copy of the instructional videotape entitled, *Grammar & Sentence Structures*.

6. Confirm that each student has purchased a copy of this Instructional Guide to document work and track progress.

7. Check all equipment before your class begins to be sure it is operational and is set up properly (VCR and monitor functional, cords placed for safety, etc.).

8. Be sure you are familiar with your classroom. Check the following:
    - Electrical outlets.
    - Entrances/exits.
    - Light switches.
    - Restroom/drinking fountain location.
    - Air conditioning/heating controls.

Room Arrangement Suggestion

For maximum visibility, a U-shaped classroom arrangement is highly recommended. The instructional methods described in this course are best employed when the room arrangement allows for full interaction among students and between the students and the instructor. Also, movable chairs are more conducive to the skill development activities provided within this course.

Consider maximum visibility when placing the VCR/Monitor. Avoid having light sources (such as a window) directly behind the monitor or light sources (such as lamps) which are reflected on the TV monitor.

When videotaping your students' work, provide a plain background which contrasts with the students' clothing. Ask students to wear clothes that contrast with skin tone. It is also recommended that you do a test video recording to ensure adequate lighting and placement.

INDEPENDENT STUDY OPTION

This non-traditional curriculum is designed to extend interpreter education for certified interpreters beyond the confines of infrequent professional development opportunities. This option is intended for interpreters that typically lack access to on-going support or for certified interpreters interested in taking charge of their own skill development. Because independent study maximizes the comfort and safety-level of learners trying new skills, it enhances the chance to learn and grow.

Learner Identification

This independent study option has been designed for:

1. Certified interpreters who want professional development opportunities while earning credits toward maintaining certification.

2. Working interpreters who wish to improve skills while endeavoring to achieve certification.

3. Interpreter educators wishing to receive CEU credit for taking this course, or for offering this course to students for the first time.

4. Advanced students of ASL who wish to enhance their understanding and application of ASL grammatical aspects.

Required Instructional Media

The same course materials are required for the independent study option as are required for classroom instruction (see Course Components). If several interpreters work on the course together for credit, each interpreter should obtain his or her own course materials.

Learner Responsibilities

The learner is responsible for following the instructions and timelines provided in this Instructional Guide. The course objectives are clearly stated in the Getting Started section, and are provided to assist in keeping the learning outcomes in focus while performing course activities. To receive credit for this course, the learner is responsible for fulfilling all the credit requirements detailed below.

Credit Requirements

This course provides instructional activities requiring up to 20 hours of professional development participation. At the completion of this course, if learners have satisfied the CMP requirements, they will be eligible for up to 2.0 CEU credits.

To receive CMP credit for this course, the following information must be submitted by the certified interpreter to an RID-approved CMP sponsor:

1. Contact an approved CMP sponsor and complete an Independent Study Activity Plan prior to beginning the course (prepared Independent Study Activity Plans for this course are available from Sign Enhancers). For a listing of approved sponsors, contact the RID at 301-608-0050.

2. The Written Assessment: The written portion must be fully completed and submitted to the approved sponsor after the completion of all ten modules.

3. The Performance Assessment: An assessment videotape must be submitted to the approved sponsor after completion of all ten modules.

4. A CMP Evaluation Form (to be obtained from the CMP-approved sponsor), along with items 2 and 3 above, must be submitted to the approved sponsor.

Timelines

Throughout this Instructional Guide, suggested timelines are recommended for each activity. Be sure you have ample time to complete the activity before beginning. To maximize learning, it is strongly recommended that a full module be completed at each session. Immediate application of new content and skills increases the chance that learning will be assimilated for long-term professional growth.

Independent Study Preparation

The following list provides a detailed, step-by-step preparation guide for the independent study learner:

1. Read this Instructional Guide, and follow all instructions in the order they appear.

2. If possible, schedule enough time to complete one full module per work session.

3. Be sure to have this Instructional Guide with you during each session to record your work and accurately execute all activities.

4. Check all equipment before your independent study session begins to be sure it is operational and set up properly (VCR and monitor functional, cords placed for safety, etc.).

5. Gather and ready all instructional supplies and equipment including:

    - This Instructional Guide.
    - Writing instrument (pen or pencil).
    - VCR for playing VHS videotape material.
    - Monitor (color preferred) for viewing videotape material.
    - Video camera for recording your work.
    - Blank VHS videotape for recording your work.

Room Arrangement Suggestion

Consider maximum visibility when placing the VCR/Monitor. Avoid having light sources (such as a window) directly behind the monitor or light sources (such as lamps) which are reflected on the TV monitor.

When videotaping your work, try to have a plain background which contrasts with your clothes. Wear clothes that contrast with your skin tone. It is also recommended that you do a test recording to ensure adequate lighting and placement. If possible, have someone assist you in aiming and focusing the videotape image.

Translation Glossing System

In each module a written script of the videotape sample sentences is provided to assist the learner in making comparisons between the original English sentence and the signed versions using ASL and PSE. Because ASL is not a written language, "glosses" are used to represent the signs and to reflect the accompanying non-manual markers (all physical expressions in Sign Language except the signs themselves).

It is important to understand that even though the glosses represent signs, there is not a one-word, one-sign equivalent between English and ASL. These glosses are not intended to provide complete linguistic information for each signed sentence. However, when used correctly, the glosses can guide you to a clearer understanding of the depth and linguistic sophistication of ASL.

Remember, the scripts provided in the modules are <u>not intended to be full gloss representations</u> of the signed sentences. They are offered as a way for you to make a comparison of English, ASL and PSE with emphasis on the grammatical topic featured in each module.

Glossing System

ALL CAPS = a gloss representing a signed concept.

Gloss	Description	Gloss	Description
(rt)	Placed or referenced to the right	(q)	Yes/no question
(lft)	Placed or referenced to the left	(rh-q)	Rhetorical question
(wh-q)	Wh-question (what, when, where...)	(t)	Topic of sentence
(CL)	Classifier	(cond)	Conditional
(CL:A)	Classifier with "A" handshape	SIGN+SIGN	Compound sign
(CL: Bent V)	Classifier with bent "V" handshape	SIGN-SIGN	One sign
me	"I," "me," indication of self	F-I-N-G-E-R-S-P-E-L-L	Fingerspelled word

Overview Summary

It is our sincere wish that this Instructional Guide, when used in conjunction with the *Grammar & Sentence Structures* videotape or CD-ROM, will provide interpreter educators with substantial support in fostering student growth. Additionally, we hope to assist interpreters and ASL students who have chosen to enhance their own skills.

By supporting educators and learners in this way, we hope to enable interpreters to positively impact their own professional lives and the lives of the consumers who will benefit from their special talents.

*You are now ready to begin...
learn well and have fun!*

COURSE 2001 Getting Started

A.1 COURSE OBJECTIVES

"Planning for Success"
10 Minutes

Activity Goal   To identify the desired learning outcomes of this course.

Activity Instructions
1. **READ** the following objectives.
2. **CONSIDER** each objective and **DETERMINE** your current knowledge and skill level regarding each item.
3. **DETERMINE** and **SET** your intention to accomplish the learning objectives in relation to your needs.

Objectives   After completing this course, learners will be able to:
1. Identify ten key linguistic features including:
    - Topic/Comment Structure
    - Yes/No Questions
    - Wh-Questions
    - Rhetorical Questions
    - Directionality
    - Use of Space
    - Negation
    - Classifiers
    - Conditionals
    - Time Sequenced Ordering
2. When given English sentences, interpret using grammatically correct ASL.
3. When given English sentences, transliterate using PSE (incorporating appropriate ASL grammatical features).
4. Accurately answer written questions pertaining to the content addressed in the course.
5. Accurately demonstrate the ten grammatical features addressed within the context of sentences.
6. Compare and contrast the ten grammatical features presented as they relate to PSE and ASL.

Instructional Guide
©1995 Sign Enhancers, Inc.

Getting Started: Pretest

A.2 PRETEST: WRITTEN PORTION

"What Do You Know?"
30 Minutes

Activity Goal   To identify the learner's current knowledge level pertaining to course content.

Activity Instructions   READ and ANSWER all questions to the best of your ability.

Learning Tip   *Remember, this is a pretest. You are not expected to respond to all questions correctly before completion of the course. Try not to be frustrated or disappointed if some of your answers are incorrect.*

1. American Sign Language (ASL) is a language complete with grammatical syntax and cultural affiliation.
    a) True
    b) False

2. Pidgin Sign English (PSE) is a language complete with grammatical syntax and cultural affiliation.
    a) True
    b) False

3. PSE is also known as (circle one):
    a) "Contact Signing"
    b) "Continual Signing"
    c) "ASL/PSE Continuum"
    d) "Combination Signing"

4. Recently, linguists have discovered that regardless of the linguistic abilities of the communicators, PSE is comprised of ASL-based signs while maintaining English grammatical structure (primarily English word order).
    a) True
    b) False

5. The appropriate non-manual features that identify the topic of a sentence in ASL include which of the following (check all that apply):
    a) ___ Eyebrow raise to identify topic.
    b) ___ Eyebrow furrow (down) to identify topic.
    c) ___ Slight head tilt forward.
    d) ___ Signer leans back.
    e) ___ Last sign identifying topic is held longer.
    f) ___ Last sign identifying topic is dropped immediately.

Getting Started: Pretest

6. The comment portion of a topic/comment structured sentence could be a (check all that apply):
   a) ___ Yes/no question
   b) ___ Wh-question
   c) ___ Statement
   d) ___ Command

7. For the following sentence, circle the topic of the sentence and underline the comment.
   Do you really want to go to that scary movie?

8. A wh-question is likely to include which of the following (check all that apply):
   a) ___ WHAT
   b) ___ HOW
   c) ___ WHO
   d) ___ WOULD
   e) ___ WHEN
   f) ___ HOW-MUCH
   g) ___ WHICHEVER

9. The appropriate non-manual features that identify a yes/no question in ASL include which of the following (check all that apply):
   a) ___ Eyebrows are raised.
   b) ___ Eyebrows are furrowed (down).
   c) ___ Head tilted slightly forward.
   d) ___ Signer leans back.
   e) ___ Last sign is held, waiting for a response.
   f) ___ Last sign identifying the question is dropped immediately so the response can be made.
   g) ___ Eye contact is made with the person being asked the question.
   h) ___ Drop eyes to indicate question is complete.

10. The non-manual grammatical markers associated with a wh-question include (check all that apply):
    a) ___ Eyebrows are raised.
    b) ___ Eyebrows are furrowed (down).
    c) ___ Head tilted slightly.
    d) ___ Eyes narrowed slightly.
    e) ___ Eyes opened wide.
    f) ___ Last sign is held, waiting for a response.
    g) ___ Last sign identifying the question is dropped immediately so the response can be made.
    h) ___ Eye contact is made with the person being asked the question.
    i) ___ Drop eyes to indicate question is complete.

11. Rhetorical questions are different than other kinds of questions because the person being "asked" the question expects the answer to be provided.
    a) True
    b) False

12. A rhetorical question's purpose is (check all that apply):
    a) ___ To show humor in communication.
    b) ___ To provide a linguistic mechanism for sarcasm.
    c) ___ To find out new information.
    d) ___ To introduce new information.
    e) ___ To show a causal relationship between two events.

Instructional Guide
©1995 Sign Enhancers, Inc.

Getting Started: Pretest

13. Which of the following verbs would you consider to be directional verbs (check all that apply):
    a) ___ LOVE
    b) ___ GIVE
    c) ___ BORROW
    d) ___ SLEEP
    e) ___ SHOW
    f) ___ LOOK
    g) ___ TEACH
    h) ___ TYPE

14. Due to the spatial features of ASL, all verbs are directional.
    a) True
    b) False

15. The method of referencing a person or persons who are not present utilizes what we call "absent referents" or "indexing." When a signer establishes and uses a referent, the eyes usually (circle one):
    a) Maintain contact with the person receiving the communication.
    b) Will gaze in the direction of the referent.
    c) Will look at the index finger as it points to the referent.
    d) Will gaze down to indicate the referent is not present.

16. Some of the sign vocabulary that might indicate a negative include (check all that apply):
    a) ___ NOT
    b) ___ DON'T
    c) ___ NO
    d) ___ CAN'T
    e) ___ WON'T

17. Signs indicating negation are sometimes not even necessary if a negative headshake is simultaneously produced with the sentence.
    a) True
    b) False

18. Classifiers are a type of sign that represent a "class" of objects. They are used in ASL to describe the movement, placement, and visual characteristics of a person or object.
    a) True
    b) False

19. A classifier composed of the thumb, index, and middle finger (CL:3) can represent which of the following vehicles (check all that apply):
    a) ___ CAR
    b) ___ AIRPLANE
    c) ___ BUS
    d) ___ TRAIN
    e) ___ SKATEBOARD
    f) ___ TRUCK
    g) ___ BICYCLE

20. In ASL, when there is a relationship between two portions of a signed discourse, such that **if** one thing occurs, **then** something else will happen, the structure is called a (circle one):
    a) "Causal"
    b) "Circumstantial"
    c) "Conditional"
    d) "Conventional"

21. For the following sentence, identify the "IF" portion of the sentence by circling it and identify the "THEN" portion by underlining it:

    I'll teach you Sign Language in exchange for washing my car.

22. An ASL user will very often give information in the same order in which it actually occurred. In the example below, indicate the order in which each event would be signed by placing the number 1 (for first), 2 (for second) or 3 (for third) next to that portion of the sentence.

    I called the police immediately when I saw the burglar break into the house.
    a) ___ I called the police immediately
    b) ___ when I saw
    c) ___ the burglar break into the house

23. When the order of sentence components follows the actual order of events, this is called (circle one):
    a) Real-time Ordering
    b) Time Sequenced Ordering
    c) Reality Sequenced Ordering
    d) Conceptual Signing

24. The term "non-manual" refers to all physical expressions in Sign Language EXCEPT the signs themselves.
    a) True
    b) False

25. In the list below, label the linguistic features applicable to ASL with an "A," the features applicable to PSE with a "P," and the features applicable to both with a "B":
    a) ___ Topic/Comment Structure
    b) ___ Rhetorical Question Format
    c) ___ Classifiers
    d) ___ Negation
    e) ___ English Structure
    f) ___ Time Sequenced Ordering
    g) ___ English Mouthing
    h) ___ Use of Space
    i) ___ Non-manual Markers

Congratulations!
You've completed the written portion of the Pretest.

A.3 Pretest: Performance Portion

"What Can You Do?"
30 Minutes

Activity Goal To identify the learner's current skill level.

Activity Instructions

1. **RECORD** pretest sentences onto an audiotape to more closely simulate the interpreting task (optional).
2. **PREPARE** room by setting up videotape camera and **VIDEOTAPE** your performance.
3. **TRANSLITERATE** each of the sentences using PSE (Contact Signing).
4. **INTERPRET** (sign using ASL) each sentence presented below, incorporating the grammatical feature listed beside each sentence.

Learning Tip *Remember, this is a pretest. You are not expected to interpret all sentences correctly before completion of the course. Try not to be frustrated or disappointed if some of your work is incorrect.*

Performance Portion Sentences	Grammatical Feature to Apply When Using ASL
1. It is important to eat breakfast every morning!	Topic/Comment
2. Are you addicted to watching TV?	Yes/No Question
3. How much did you pay for your car?	Wh-Question
4. I was just hired because I have 15 years of work experience.	Rh-Question
5. I need help because my car broke down.	Directionality
6. Who is that red-headed girl?	Use of Space
7. I can't find my glasses!	Negation
8. The man walked as if he were drunk.	Classifier
9. My boss will fire me if I call in sick again.	Conditional
10. I'm tired because I've been working hard all day after getting up so early this morning.	Time Sequenced Ordering

A.4 Mini-Lecture

"What is ASL?"
10 Minutes

Activity Goal — To comprehend the signed lecture and to identify information pertaining to American Sign Language.

Activity Instructions

1. **VIEW** the mini-lecture provided by Nathie Marbury <u>without</u> sound or closed captions.
2. **SUMMARIZE** the mini-lecture in the space allotted below.
3. **CHECK** your understanding by **REPLAYING** the segment, this time with the sound/captions turned on (optional).

Mini-Lecture Summary

_____
_____
_____
_____
_____
_____
_____
_____
_____
_____

A.5 Linguistic Information

"Introduction to ASL"
10 Minutes

Goal — To provide the learner with a knowledge base that supports the learning experience.

Instructions
1. **READ** the following information defining American Sign Language.
2. **NOTE** any new information.

Introduction To American Sign Language

American Sign Language

American Sign Language (ASL) is a language complete with grammatical syntax and cultural affiliation. Members of the American Deaf Culture consider ASL their native language.

Like spoken languages, such as French and Spanish, ASL is a distinct language with a set of complex grammatical rules.

Although ASL is not a written language, many states in the U.S. have accepted it as a formal language, and offer ASL as a way to meet second language requirements in high schools and universities.

As with any language, ASL is intimately tied to its culture. Deaf cultural members value their language highly, and take pride in the beauty and efficiency of ASL.

ASL is a language distinct and separate from English. The grammatical structure is more similar to French than English because of ASL's history and origin from France.

A.6 Mini-Lecture

"What is PSE?"
10 Minutes

Activity Goal To comprehend the signed lecture and to identify information pertaining to Pidgin Sign English.

Activity Instructions

1. **VIEW** the mini-lecture provided by Nathie Marbury <u>without</u> sound or closed captions.

2. **SUMMARIZE** the mini-lecture in the space allotted below.

3. **CHECK** your understanding by **REPLAYING** the segment, this time with the sound/captions turned on (optional).

Mini-Lecture Summary

_____
_____
_____
_____
_____
_____
_____
_____
_____
_____
_____
_____
_____

A.7 Linguistic Information

"Introduction to PSE"
10 Minutes

Goal To provide the learner with a knowledge base that supports the learning experience.

Instructions
1. **READ** the following information pertaining to Pidgin Sign English.
2. **NOTE** any new information.

Introduction to PSE Throughout the world, the term "pidgin" is used to describe what generally occurs when two or more persons from different cultures try to communicate.

For example, a Spanish-speaking person may understand only one English word, such as "bathroom." An American tourist desperately seeking the location of these facilities may know only one Spanish word, such as "donde'" (meaning "where"). When the tourist approaches the Spanish speaking person, his panicked question may be "Donde' bathroom?" Although this is not grammatically correct in either language, the resulting pidgin is intelligible, and the communication is successful . . . to the great relief of the tourist!

A pidgin typically combines elements of both vocabulary and grammar from each of the communicators' languages. The amount of each language incorporated depends upon the communicators' relative fluencies.

Pidgin Sign English (PSE), also known as "Contact Signing," combines features of both ASL and English. In any given situation, the relative amounts of each language depends on the fluency and preferences of the communicators. Typically, PSE is comprised of ASL-based signs while using elements of English grammatical structure, especially word order.

The incorporation of ASL grammatical features into PSE communication varies from signer to signer. This course will assist you in identifying ways to incorporate many of the grammatical aspects of ASL when using PSE as a way to better match the preferences of consumers requesting transliteration.

Congratulations!

You've successfully completed the Getting Started section, and are ready to proceed to the ten instructional modules!

Have fun while enhancing your skills!

MODULE 1: Topic/Comment Structure

1.1 Mini-Lecture
10 Minutes

Activity Goal To comprehend the signed lecture and to identify the main characteristics involved in producing sentences using topic/comment structure.

Activity Instructions

1. **VIEW** the mini-lecture provided by Nathie Marbury <u>without</u> sound or closed captions.

2. **SUMMARIZE** the mini-lecture in the space allotted below.

3. **CHECK** your understanding by **REPLAYING** the segment, this time with the sound/captions turned on (optional).

Mini-Lecture Summary

_____

_____

_____

_____

_____

_____

_____

_____

_____

_____

Instructional Guide
©1995 Sign Enhancers, Inc.

1.2 Linguistic Information
10 Minutes

Activity Goal To provide the learner with a knowledge base that supports the learning experience.

Activity Instructions
1. **READ** the following information pertaining to topic/comment structure.
2. **NOTE** any new information.

Linguistic Topic

Topic/Comment Structure

In ASL, ideas are commonly ordered using "topic/comment structure." This means that the topic (what the sentence is talking about) is identified first. This topic is signed first with the following accompanying non-manual grammatical markers:

- Eyebrow raise.
- Slight head tilt forward.
- Last sign identifying topic is held longer.

Notice how these markers resemble the "questioning markers." This questioning seems to ask the communication recipient if they understand what the topic is.

Just as the topic in topic/comment structure is accompanied by these questioning markers, the comment is also accompanied by one of the following non-manual grammatical markers:

- <u>Yes/no question markers</u> appear if the comment asks a question eliciting a "yes" or "no" response. The non-manual grammatical markers that accompany such a question are:
  - Eyebrows raised.
  - Head tilted slightly forward.
  - Eye contact made with the person being asked the question.
  - The last sign held, waiting for a response.

Example

English sentence: Do you want milk?
ASL sentence: MILK (t), WANT (you) (q)

Module 1: Topic/Comment Structure

- Wh-question markers are used if the comment asks a question about who, what, where, when, which, how, why, etc. The non-manual grammatical markers that accompany such a question are:

    - Eyebrows furrowed (down).
    - Eyes narrowed slightly.
    - Head tilted slightly.
    - Eye contact made with the person being asked the question.
    - The last sign held, waiting for a response.

    ### Example

    English sentence: Where is Tom?
    ASL sentence: TOM (t), WHERE (wh-q)

- Statement markers are used if the comment is a statement about the topic. The markers that accompany a statement are:

    - The head returns to an upright position from the "slight forward lean."
    - The head often nods affirmatively to emphasize that the comment is a statement.

    ### Example

    English sentence: I love trees.
    ASL sentence: TREES (t), LOVE (me)

- Command markers are used if the comment is a command. The non-manual grammatical markers that accompany a command are:

    - The head returns to an upright position from the "slight forward lean."
    - The head often nods once to emphasize that the comment is a command.
    - Often, a stern facial expression will accompany the entire comment.

    ### Example

    English sentence: Go home!
    ASL sentence: HOME (t), GO THERE (rt)

Module 1: Topic/Comment Structure

1.3 Instructional Activity

"What's It All About?"
10 Minutes

Activity Goals
1. To practice identifying the topic and comment within written English sentences as preparation for interpreting using topic/comment structure.
2. To compare topic/comment structure in ASL with the structure commonly associated with PSE.

Activity Instructions

1. **READ** the following sentences to determine the topic and comment within each sentence.
2. **IDENTIFY** the topic of the sentence by **CIRCLING** the entire topic.
3. **IDENTIFY** the comment of the sentence by **UNDERLINING** that portion of the sentence.
4. **INDICATE** whether the grammatical order would be the same or different if you were to sign the same sentence using PSE by checking Same or Different.
5. **CHECK** your answers by viewing the model signers on the companion video.

Learning Tip   *A good way to determine the topic of a sentence is to ask yourself, "What is this sentence about?" A good way to find the comment is to ask yourself, "What is being said or asked about that topic?"*

Example

Topic circled. Comment underlined.	The ASL & PSE grammatical structures are:
I love (my mother!) [I love underlined, my mother! circled]	__Same ✔ Different

Activity Sentences
1. (My daughter) is smart.   ✓ Same __Different
2. (Where) is my telephone book?   __Same ✓ Different
3. It is important to (eat) breakfast every morning!   __Same ✓ Different
4. What is your phone number?   __Same ✓ Different

Module 1: Topic/Comment Structure

5. Can you postpone my appointment?   __Same ✓Different

6. My favorite thing to do is go shopping.   ✓Same __Different

7. That man is famous because he used to be the U.S. president!   ✓Same __Different

8. I like working on the farm.   __Same ✓Different

9. Who is your divorce lawyer?   __Same ✓Different

10. I really like your picture!   __Same ✓Different

11. I want lunch now.   __Same ✓Different

Module 1: Topic/Comment Structure

1.4 Video Practice Activity

"Interpreting & Transliterating Skill Development"
30 Minutes

Activity Goal — To practice transliterating using PSE and practice interpreting using ASL while learning from the models presented on the videotape.

Activity Instructions

1. **BEGIN** videotaped segment that demonstrates topic/comment structure in the sample sentences.

2. **VIEW** written sentence on the screen, **STOP TAPE** by hitting the pause button.

3. **PRACTICE** transliterating the sentence using PSE.

4. **PLAY VIDEO** and **VIEW** model. **COMPARE** PSE rendition to your transliteration.

5. **PLAY VIDEO** and **REREAD** written sentence. **HIT PAUSE** button.

6. **PRACTICE INTERPRETING** the sentence using ASL.

Learning Tip — *As you practice formulating your interpretation for each sentence, remember to apply topic/comment structure as addressed in this section.*

7. **PLAY VIDEO** and **VIEW** model. **COMPARE** ASL rendition to your interpretation.

8. **REPEAT** steps 1-7 for each sentence, incorporating the skills you have learned from the models.

9. **REVIEW** the sentences once more to **COMPARE AND CONTRAST** the ASL and PSE renditions of the models for:
   - Word/sign order.
   - Non-manual grammatical features.
   - Vocabulary/sign choices.

1.5 Module Review

"Topic/Comment Structure"
30 Minutes

Activity Goal To review the information provided within this module by producing each sample sentence using PSE and ASL.

Activity Instructions

1. **REVIEW** section 1.2 Linguistic Information.
2. **REVIEW** the sample sentences from the videotape segment in this section.
3. **READ** each of the English sentences provided in the section below and **APPLY** what you have learned by **PRODUCING** each sentence first using PSE, then ASL.
4. **CHECK** your work by referring to the glosses provided in the following section.

Learning Tip *It is recommended that you videotape your work. Compare your signed renditions to that of the models on the videotape.*

Activity Sentences

1. I love my mother!
2. My daughter is very smart.
3. Where is my telephone book?
4. It is important to eat breakfast every morning!
5. What is your phone number?
6. Can you postpone my appointment?
7. My favorite thing to do is go shopping.
8. That man is famous because he used to be the U.S. president!
9. I like working on the farm.
10. Who is your divorce lawyer?
11. I really like your picture!
12. I want lunch now.

Comparative Translations

1. *English Sentence:* I love my mother!
   PSE Gloss: ME LOVE MY MOTHER
   ASL Gloss: MY MOTHER (t) ME LOVE

2. *English Sentence:* My daughter is very smart.
   PSE Gloss: MY DAUGHTER VERY SMART
   ASL Gloss: MY DAUGHTER (t), VERY-SMART

3. *English Sentence:* Where is my telephone book?
   PSE Gloss: WHERE MY TELEPHONE BOOK (wh-q)
   ASL Gloss: MY TELEPHONE BOOK (t), WHERE (wh-q)

4. *English Sentence:* It is important to eat breakfast every morning!
   PSE Gloss: TRUE IMPORTANT, EAT EVERY-MORNING
   ASL Gloss: EVERY-MORNING, EAT+EAT (t), IMPORTANT

5. *English Sentence:* What is your phone number?
   PSE Gloss: WHAT YOUR PHONE NUMBER (wh-q)
   ASL Gloss: YOUR PHONE NUMBER (t), WHAT (wh-q)

6. *English Sentence:* Can you postpone my appointment?
   PSE Gloss: CAN YOU POSTPONE MY APPOINTMENT (q)
   ASL Gloss: MY APPOINTMENT (t), POSTPONE, CAN (q)

7. *English Sentence:* My favorite thing to do is go shopping.
   PSE Gloss: MY FAVORITE THING DO, GO SHOP+SHOP
   ASL Gloss: SHOP+SHOP (t), ME LOVE

8.	*English Sentence:*	That man is famous because he used to be the U.S. president!
	PSE Gloss:	THAT MAN (rt) FAMOUS BECAUSE PAST U.S. PRESIDENT
	ASL Gloss:	THAT MAN (rt) (t) FAMOUS, NAME-SHINY, WHY (rh-q), PAST PRESIDENT HERE AMERICA
9.	*English Sentence:*	I like working on the farm.
	PSE Gloss:	I LIKE WORK THERE-(rt) FARM
	ASL Gloss:	FARM (t), ME WORK+WORK +WORK, ME LIKE (KISS-FIST)
10.	*English Sentence:*	Who is your divorce lawyer?
	PSE Gloss:	WHO YOUR DIVORCE LAWYER (wh-q)
	ASL Gloss:	YOUR DIVORCE LAWYER (t), WHO (wh-q)
11.	*English Sentence:*	I really like your picture!
	PSE Gloss:	I TRUE LIKE YOUR PICTURE
	ASL Gloss:	YOUR PICTURE (t) (rt), ME REALLY-LIKE
12.	*English Sentence:*	I want lunch now.
	PSE Gloss:	ME WANT EAT+NOON NOW
	ASL Gloss:	EAT+NOON (t), ME WANT NOW

Module 1: Topic/Comment Structure

1.6 Skills Application

"Topic/Comment Structure"
15 Minutes

Activity Goal — To practice applying topic/comment structure to new stimuli.

Activity Instructions

1. **PRACTICE** applying the information and skills you have learned in this module by **INTERPRETING** the following new sentences **USING** topic/comment structure.

2. **APPLY** the non-manual markers associated with producing an ASL sentence using topic/comment structure.

3. **PRACTICE** transliterating each sentence. **COMPARE** the grammatical structure and non-manual markers to your ASL interpretations.

Learning Tips

1. *You can record these sentences onto an audiotape to more closely simulate a voice-to-sign interpreting situation.*

2. *It is recommended that you videotape your work.*

Activity Sentences

1. Give me the tall blue glass.
2. Tom's car is very beautiful.
3. I need gas now!
4. That tree is very old.
5. I really want to go to college.
6. Are you fluent in Sign Language?
7. My bed is so comfortable.
8. Who is your secretary?
9. Sally jumped into the swimming pool.
10. I bought many new clothes.

Congratulations!
You have completed Module One!

MODULE 2: Yes/No Questions

2.1 MINI-LECTURE
10 Minutes

Activity Goal   To comprehend the signed lecture and to identify the main characteristics involved in producing yes/no questions.

Activity Instructions

1. **VIEW** the mini-lecture provided by Nathie Marbury <u>without</u> sound or closed captions.
2. **SUMMARIZE** the mini-lecture in the space allotted below.
3. **CHECK** your understanding by **REPLAYING** the segment, this time with the sound/captions turned on (optional).

Mini-Lecture Summary

_____

_____

_____

_____

_____

_____

_____

_____

_____

_____

2.2 Linguistic Information
10 Minutes

Activity Goal — To provide the learner with a knowledge base that supports the learning experience.

Activity Instructions
1. **READ** the following information pertaining to yes/no question format.
2. **NOTE** any new information.

Linguistic Topic

Yes/No Questions

In ASL, questions that require a "yes" or "no" response are referred to as "yes/no questions." These questions are accompanied by the following non-manual grammatical markers:

- Eyebrows are raised.
- Head tilted slightly forward.
- Eye contact is made with the person being asked the question.
- The last sign is held, waiting for a response.

Examples of yes/no questions:

- Do you want to go to a movie?
- Do you like Tom?
- Will you come home now?
- Are you married?

Notice that each of the above questions would elicit a "yes" or "no" response.

In written English, the question format is demonstrated with the use of a question mark (?). In spoken English, the question format is indicated by the use of vocal inflection. Most often, the voice will go up in pitch to indicate a "yes" or "no" question.

A manual "questioning" marker that is particular to yes/no questions and to wh-questions is the "question finger." This is produced with the index finger in a "one" handshape which bends and straightens several times in the direction of the person being asked the question. This is often done to show that the signer is waiting for a response. The manual "questioning" marker is optional, whereas the non-manual grammatical markers previously described *must* accompany every question.

2.3 Instructional Activity

"Yes or No, That is the Question Format!"
5 Minutes

Activity Goal To distinguish yes/no questions from other question forms.

Activity Instructions CHECK the sentence representing the yes/no question in each set of sentences below.

Activity Sentences

Question #1

a) ____ Where does your mother live?
b) ____ Does your mother live in Arizona?
c) ____ My mother lives in Arizona.

Question #2

a) ____ Do you have a TTY?
b) ____ Why do you have a TTY?
c) ____ I have a TTY.

Question #3

a) ____ Why didn't you have enough to eat?
b) ____ I did not have enough to eat.
c) ____ Did you have enough to eat?

Question #4

a) ____ Where is your home?
b) ____ Do you want to go home?
c) ____ How will you get home?

Question #5

a) ____ Do you want a drink?
b) ____ Did you want a pepsi or a coke?
c) ____ How thirsty are you?

Question #6

a) ____ When will you finish working?
b) ____ How much more work do you have?
c) ____ Is your work completed?

Module 2: Yes/No Questions

2.4 Video Practice Activity

"Interpreting & Transliterating Skill Development"
30 Minutes

Activity Goal To practice transliterating using PSE and practice interpreting using ASL while learning from the models presented on the videotape.

Activity Instructions

1. **BEGIN** videotaped segment that demonstrates yes/no questions in the sample sentences.

2. **VIEW** written sentence on the screen, **STOP TAPE** by hitting the pause button.

3. **PRACTICE** transliterating the sentence using PSE.

4. **PLAY VIDEO** and **VIEW** model. **COMPARE** PSE rendition to your transliteration.

5. **PLAY VIDEO** and **REREAD** written sentence. **HIT PAUSE** button.

6. **PRACTICE INTERPRETING** the sentence using ASL.

Learning Tip *As you practice formulating your interpretation for each sentence, remember to apply yes/no questions as addressed in this section.*

7. **PLAY VIDEO** and **VIEW** model. **COMPARE** ASL rendition to your interpretation.

8. **REPEAT** steps 1-7 for each sentence, incorporating the skills you have learned from the models.

9. **REVIEW** the sentences once more to **COMPARE AND CONTRAST** the ASL and PSE renditions of the models for:

    - Word/sign order.
    - Non-manual grammatical features.
    - Vocabulary/sign choices.

Module 2: Yes/No Questions

2.5 Instructional Activity

"Are You Raising Your Brows at Me?"
10 Minutes

Activity Goal To compare the non-manual grammatical markers of PSE and ASL sentences when producing yes/no questions.

Activity Instructions

1. **VIEW** each sample sentence on the videotape in the yes/no questions topic area.
2. **NOTE** and **COMPARE** the non-manual markers in the PSE and ASL sentences.
3. **CHECK** whether the non-manuals indicating yes/no questions are the same or different when using ASL and PSE.

Learning Tip *Remember, the way to ask a yes/no question incorporates the following non-manual grammatical features:*
- *Brow raise.*
- *Eye contact.*
- *Head tilt.*
- *Holding the last sign while waiting for a response.*

Example

The non-manual markers include: brow raise, eye contact, head tilt and last sign held in both ASL and PSE.	The ASL and PSE non-manual markers are:
Are you Deaf?	✓ Same __ Different

Activity Sentences

1. Do you have a car? __Same __Different
2. Do you want a soda? __Same __Different
3. Can you come here when you are finished eating? __Same __Different
4. Are you hearing? __Same __Different
5. Do you want to go to a restaurant tonight? __Same __Different
6. Do you have a TTY? __Same __Different
7. Are you addicted to watching TV? __Same __Different
8. Did you see the accident? __Same __Different
9. Did you have enough to eat? __Same __Different

Instructional Guide
©1995 Sign Enhancers, Inc.

Module 2: Yes/No Questions

10. You look sleepy, do you want some coffee to help you wake up? __Same __Different

2.6 Instructional Activity

"It's Only a Drill!"
10 Minutes

Activity Goal To incorporate ASL grammatical structure and the non-manual markers for producing yes/no questions with the introduction of new stimulus vocabulary.

Activity Instructions
1. **READ** the original yes/no question.
2. **REPLACE** the underlined vocabulary item with the next item in the list. If you do this exercise using ASL, remember to retain ASL grammatical structure, including the non-manual markers.

Practice Drill
1. Did you see the <u>accident</u>?
    burning house
    deer cross the road
    woman fall down
    new freeway

2. Did you have enough <u>to eat</u>?
    money
    clothes
    milk
    gas

3. Are you <u>addicted to</u> watching TV?
    mesmerized by
    enjoying
    adverse to
    in favor of

4. Do you want to go to <u>a restaurant</u> <u>tonight</u>?
    a rodeo   next month
    the beach   next week

Instructional Guide
©1995 Sign Enhancers, Inc.

2.7 Module Review

"Yes/No Questions"
30 Minutes

Activity Goal   To review the information provided within this module by producing each sample sentence using ASL and PSE.

Activity Instructions
1. **REVIEW** section 2.2 Linguistic Information.
2. **REVIEW** the sample sentences from the videotape segment in this section.
3. **READ** each of the English sentences provided in the section below and **APPLY** what you have learned by **PRODUCING** each sentence first using PSE, then ASL.
4. **CHECK** your work by referring to the glosses provided in the following section.

Learning Tip   *It is recommended that you videotape your work. Compare your signed renditions to that of the models on the videotape.*

Activity Sentences
1. Are you Deaf?
2. Do you have a car?
3. Do you want a soda?
4. Can you come here when you are finished eating?
5. Are you hearing?
6. Do you want to go to a restaurant tonight?
7. Do you have a TTY?
8. Are you addicted to watching TV?
9. Did you see the accident?
10. Did you have enough to eat?
11. You look sleepy, do you want some coffee to help you wake up?

Module 2: Yes/No Questions

Comparative Translations

1. *English Sentence:* Are you Deaf?
   PSE Gloss: YOU DEAF (q)
   ASL Gloss: DEAF, YOU (q)

2. *English Sentence:* Do you have a car?
   PSE Gloss: YOU HAVE CAR (q)
   ASL Gloss: CAR (t), HAVE YOU (q)

3. *English Sentence:* Do you want a soda?
   PSE Gloss: YOU WANT SODA (q)
   ASL Gloss: SODA (t), DRINK YOU WANT (q)

4. *English Sentence:* Can you come here when you are finished eating?
   PSE Gloss: CAN YOU COME HERE WHEN YOU FINISH EAT+EAT (q)
   ASL Gloss: EAT FINISH, COME-HERE CAN (q)

5. *English Sentence:* Are you hearing?
   PSE Gloss: TRUE YOU HEARING (q)
   ASL Gloss: HEARING YOU (q)

6. *English Sentence:* Do you want to go to a restaurant tonight?
   PSE Gloss: YOU WANT GO (lft) RESTAURANT TONIGHT (q)
   ASL Gloss: TONIGHT, RESTAURANT GO (lft), WANT (q)

7. *English Sentence:* Do you have a TTY?
   PSE Gloss: YOU HAVE TTY (q)
   ASL Gloss: TTY (t), HAVE YOU (q)

8. *English Sentence:* Are you addicted to watching TV?
   PSE Gloss: YOU ADDICT WATCH (rt) TV (q)
   ASL Gloss: TV, YOU WATCH, WATCH (rt), ADDICT YOU (q)

9. *English Sentence:* Did you see the accident?
   PSE Gloss: YOU SEE (lft) ACCIDENT (q)
   ASL Gloss: ACCIDENT (t) (lft), SEE FINISH (q)

10. *English Sentence:* Did you have enough to eat?
    PSE Gloss: YOU HAVE ENOUGH EAT (q)
    ASL Gloss: EAT FINISH, SATISFY (q)

	11. *English Sentence:*	You look sleepy, do you want some coffee to help you wake up?
	PSE Gloss:	YOU LOOK SLEEPY, YOU WANT SOME COFFEE (q) HELP-YOU WAKE-UP
	ASL Gloss:	SEEM EYELIDS HEAVY, YOU, COFFEE (t), WANT (q) HELP WAKE-UP, WILL

2.8 Skills Application

"Yes/No Questions"
15 Minutes

Activity Goal To practice applying the yes/no question format to new stimuli.

Activity Instructions
1. **PRACTICE** applying the information and skills you have learned in this module by **INTERPRETING** the following sentences **USING** yes/no questions.
2. **APPLY** the non-manual markers associated with producing an ASL sentence using yes/no questions.
3. **PRACTICE** transliterating each sentence. **COMPARE** the grammatical structure and non-manual markers to your ASL interpretations.

Learning Tips
1. *You can record these sentences onto an audiotape to more closely simulate a voice-to-sign interpreting situation.*
2. *It is recommended that you videotape your work.*

Activity Sentences
1. Are you going to your mother's house?
2. Is that book yours?
3. Can I drive your car?
4. Did you buy the picture?
5. Is someone sitting in this chair?
6. Would it be all right if I call you later?
7. Do you want a hamburger?
8. Are you still sick?
9. Do you work here?
10. Are you happy?

Congratulations!
You have completed Module Two!

MODULE 3: Wh-Questions

3.1 Mini-Lecture

Note: There is not a mini-lecture on the videotape for this wh-question module. See 3.2 Linguistic Information below to learn more about wh-questions.

3.2 Linguistic Information
5 Minutes

Activity Goal To provide the learner with a knowledge base that supports the learning experience.

Activity Instructions
1. **READ** the following information pertaining to wh-questions.
2. **NOTE** any new information.

Linguistic Topic Wh-Questions

In ASL, questions referring to who, what, which, where, when, why, how, etc. are called "wh-questions." A question in this form is also accompanied by the following non-manual grammatical markers called "wh-questioning markers:"

- Eyebrows are furrowed (down).
- Eyes are narrowed slightly.
- Head tilted slightly.
- Eye contact is made with the person being asked the question.
- The last sign is held, waiting for a response.

Examples of "wh-questions:"
- Who is going to the movie?
- Where is Tom?
- When will you be coming home?
- Why are you leaving?
- How much money do you have?

You will view the sample sentences on the videotape in the next activity to see wh-questions demonstrated by the signing models.

Module 3: Wh-Questions

3.3 Instructional Activity

"What Do You Know About Wh-Questions?"
20 Minutes

Activity Goal To compare use of wh-question format within PSE and ASL to enable the learner to apply this grammatical feature during future interpreting and transliterating work.

Activity Instructions

1. **VIEW** each signed wh-question sample sentence on the videotape.

2. **NOTE** the signs used in each of the PSE and ASL sample sentences that indicate a wh-question.

3. **NOTE** the non-manual markers used in producing the wh-questions within each of the PSE and ASL sample sentences.

4. Given the above information, **COMPLETE** the statements below with the most appropriate response.

Statements

1. Typically, the signs used to indicate a wh-question include:

   _____

   _____

   _____

2. In the ASL sentence samples, the indicators of a wh-question (wh-signs and non-manual markers) are typically found at the (circle one):
   beginning, middle, or end of the sentence.

3. In the PSE sentence samples, the indicators of a wh-question (wh-signs and non-manual markers) are typically found at the (circle one):
   beginning, middle, or end of the sentence.

Instructional Guide
©1995 Sign Enhancers, Inc.

Module 3: Wh-Questions

4. In the ASL sentence samples, the following non-manual grammatical markers are used in producing wh-questions (check all that apply):

   a) __ Eyebrows furrowed (down).

   b) __ Eyes narrowed slightly.

   c) __ Head tilted slightly.

   d) __ Eye contact made with the person being asked the question.

   e) __ The last sign held waiting for a response.

5. In the PSE sentence samples, the following non-manual grammatical markers are used in producing wh-questions: (check all that apply.)

   a) __ Eyebrows furrowed (down).

   b) __ Eyes narrowed slightly.

   c) __ Head tilted slightly.

   d) __ Eye contact made with the person being asked the question.

   e) __ The last sign held waiting for a response.

3.4 Video Practice Activity

"Interpreting & Transliterating Skill Development"
30 Minutes

Activity Goal To practice transliterating using PSE and practice interpreting using ASL while learning from the models presented on the videotape.

Activity Instructions

1. **BEGIN** videotaped segment that demonstrates wh-questions in the sample sentences.

2. **VIEW** written sentence on the screen, **STOP TAPE** by hitting the pause button.

3. **PRACTICE** transliterating the sentence using PSE.

4. **PLAY VIDEO** and **VIEW** model. **COMPARE** PSE rendition to your transliteration.

5. **PLAY VIDEO** and **REREAD** written sentence. **HIT PAUSE** button.

6. **PRACTICE INTERPRETING** the sentence using ASL.

Learning Tip *As you practice formulating your interpretation for each sentence, remember to apply wh-questions as addressed in this section.*

7. **PLAY VIDEO** and **VIEW** model. **COMPARE** ASL rendition to your interpretation.

8. **REPEAT** steps 1-7 for each sentence, incorporating the skills you have learned from the models.

9. **REVIEW** the sentences once more to **COMPARE AND CONTRAST** the ASL and PSE renditions of the models for:

   - Word/sign order.
   - Non-manual grammatical features.
   - Vocabulary/sign choices.

Module 3: Wh-Questions

3.5 Module Review

"Wh-Questions"
30 Minutes

Activity Goal To review the information provided within this module by producing each sample sentence using ASL and PSE.

Activity Instructions

1. **REVIEW** section 3.2 Linguistic Information.
2. **REVIEW** the sample sentences from the videotape segment in this section.
3. **READ** each of the English sentences provided in the section below and **APPLY** what you have learned by **PRODUCING** each sentence first using PSE, then ASL.
4. **CHECK** your work by referring to the glosses provided in the following section.

Learning Tip *It is recommended that you videotape your work. Compare your signed renditions to that of the models on the videotape.*

Activity Sentences
1. Who is your piano teacher?
2. Which school do you attend?
3. Where do you live?
4. How did you hurt your arm?
5. What kind of work do you do?
6. How much did you pay for your car?
7. How many children do you have?
8. What time does the airplane leave?
9. When will you have your wedding?
10. Where is my blue book?
11. How did you learn to sign so well?
12. When will your dad get home?
13. Where is the bathroom?
14. Which car did you buy?
15. Where did you learn to sign and fingerspell?

Comparative Translations

1. *English Sentence:* Who is your piano teacher?
   PSE Gloss: WHO YOUR PIANO TEACHER (wh-q)
   ASL Gloss: YOUR PIANO TEACHER (t), WHO (wh-q)

2. *English Sentence:* Which school do you attend?
   PSE Gloss: WHICH SCHOOL YOU GO (lft) (wh-q)
   ASL Gloss: SCHOOL (t), YOU GO (rt), WHICH (wh-q)

3. *English Sentence:* Where do you live?
   PSE Gloss: WHERE YOU LIVE (wh-q)
   ASL Gloss: LIVE, WHERE YOU (wh-q)

4. *English Sentence:* How did you hurt your arm?
   PSE Gloss: HOW YOU HURT YOUR ARM (wh-q)
   ASL Gloss: YOUR ARM HURT (t), HOW (wh-q)

5. *English Sentence:* What kind of work do you do?
   PSE Gloss: WHAT KIND WORK YOU DO (wh-q)
   ASL Gloss: WORK YOU (t), DO-DO-DO (wh-q)

6. *English Sentence:* How much did you pay for your car?
   PSE Gloss: HOW-MUCH YOU SPEND (rt) FOR YOUR CAR (wh-q)
   ASL Gloss: YOUR CAR (t), YOU SPEND (rt) HOW-MUCH (wh-q)

7. *English Sentence:* How many children do you have?
   PSE Gloss: HOW-MANY CHILDREN YOU HAVE (wh-q)
   ASL Gloss: CHILDREN (t), HOW-MANY HAVE (wh-q)

8. *English Sentence:* What time does the airplane leave?
   PSE Gloss: WHAT TIME AIRPLANE LEAVE (wh-q)
   ASL Gloss: AIRPLANE (t) TAKE-OFF (rt), TIME (wh-q)

9. *English Sentence:* When will you have your wedding?
   PSE Gloss: WHEN WILL YOU HAVE YOUR WEDDING (wh-q)
   ASL Gloss: YOUR WEDDING (t), WHEN (wh-q)

10. *English Sentence:* Where is my blue book?
    PSE Gloss: WHERE MY BLUE BOOK (wh-q)
    ASL Gloss: MY BOOK, BLUE (t), WHERE (wh-q)

11. *English Sentence:* How did you learn to sign so well?
    PSE Gloss: HOW YOU LEARN SIGN GOOD (wh-q)
    ASL Gloss: YOU SIGN, SIGN, EXPERT... LEARN, HOW (wh-q)

12. *English Sentence:* When will your dad get home?
    PSE Gloss: WHEN YOUR DAD ARRIVE HOME (wh-q)
    ASL Gloss: YOUR DAD ARRIVE HOME (t), WHEN (wh-q)

13. *English Sentence:* Where is the bathroom?
    PSE Gloss: WHERE BATHROOM (wh-q)
    ASL Gloss: BATHROOM (t), WHERE (wh-q)

14. *English Sentence:* Which car did you buy?
    PSE Gloss: WHICH CAR YOU BUY (wh-q)
    ASL Gloss: CAR (t), BUY WHICH (wh-q)

15. *English Sentence:* Where did you learn to sign and fingerspell?
    PSE Gloss: WHERE YOU LEARN SIGN AND FINGERSPELL (wh-q)
    ASL Gloss: YOU SIGN, FINGERSPELL, LEARN WHERE (wh-q)

Module 3: Wh-Questions

3.6 Skills Application

"Wh-Questions"
15 Minutes

Activity Goal To practice applying the wh-question format to new stimuli.

Activity Instructions

1. **PRACTICE** applying the information and skills you have learned in this module by **INTERPRETING** the following sentences **USING** wh-questions.

2. **APPLY** the non-manual markers associated with producing an ASL sentence using wh-questions.

3. **PRACTICE** transliterating each sentence. **COMPARE** the grammatical structure and non-manual markers to your ASL interpretations.

Learning Tips

1. *You can record these sentences onto an audiotape to more closely simulate a voice-to-sign interpreting situation.*

2. *It is recommended that you videotape your work.*

Activity Sentences

1. What's wrong with the teacher?
2. Where is my coat?
3. Which room is Jeff in?
4. Who will do all this work?
5. When is the plane supposed to land?
6. Why is Kim crying?
7. Did you want a soda or milk?
8. Which TV program do you like?
9. How many students are late?
10. How much does that bicycle cost?

Congratulations!
You have completed Module Three!

MODULE 4: Rhetorical Questions

4.1 Mini-Lecture
10 Minutes

Activity Goal To comprehend the signed lecture and to identify the main characteristics involved in producing rhetorical questions.

Activity Instructions

1. **VIEW** the mini-lecture provided by Nathie Marbury <u>without</u> sound or closed captions.

2. **SUMMARIZE** the mini-lecture in the space allotted below.

3. **CHECK** your understanding by **REPLAYING** the segment, this time with the sound/captions turned on (optional).

Mini-Lecture Summary

_____
_____
_____
_____
_____
_____
_____
_____
_____
_____

Module 4: Rhetorical Questions

4.2 Linguistic Information
10 Minutes

Activity Goal To provide the learner with a knowledge base that supports the learning experience.

Activity Instructions
1. **READ** the following information pertaining to rhetorical questions.
2. **NOTE** any new information.

Linguistic Topic

Rhetorical Questions

In ASL, rhetorical questions are question formats in which both the "question" and the "answer" are provided by the signer.

Actually, rhetorical questions function like statements. A rhetorical question is identified by the following non-manual grammatical markers accompanying the question portion:

- Head tilted slightly to the side.
- Eyebrows raised.
- Last sign in the question segment held slightly.

Because rhetorical questions often use the signs WHAT, WHERE, WHEN, WHICH, HOW and WHY, they are easily identifiable by the brow raise. This marker clearly notifies the receiver of the "question" and that no response is required. In fact, this non-manual grammatical feature can be used without a wh-question sign.

The non-manual grammatical markers that accompany the "response" portion of the rhetorical question are identical to those used in statement markers, including:

- The head returns to an upright position.
- The head often nods affirmatively.

Rhetorical questions are generally used in ASL to introduce new information. Here are some examples:

- ME WORK WHERE (rh-q), SIGN ENHANCERS
- MY NAME WHAT (rh-q), JERRY
- ME LIVE WHERE (rh-q), 4 MAIN STREET
- MY GRANDFATHER OLD (rh-q), 97

Instructional Guide
©1995 *Sign Enhancers, Inc.*

Module 4: Rhetorical Questions

Rhetorical questions are also used to show a causal relationship between two events. Here are some examples:

- ME HAPPY, WHY (rh-q), YOU HERE
- LITTLE GIRL SCARED, WHY (rh-q), ROOM DARK
- TOM ARRIVE HOME, HOW (rh-q), C-A-B

In summary, questions that function like statements and introduce information or show a causal relationship are called what? . . . Rhetorical questions!

4.3 Video Practice Activity

"Interpreting & Transliterating Skill Development"
30 Minutes

Activity Goal To practice transliterating using PSE and practice interpreting using ASL while learning from the models presented on the videotape.

Activity Instructions

1. **BEGIN** videotaped segment that demonstrates rh-questions in the sample sentences.
2. **VIEW** written sentence on the screen, **STOP TAPE** by hitting the pause button.
3. **PRACTICE** transliterating the sentence using PSE.
4. **PLAY VIDEO** and **VIEW** model. **COMPARE** PSE rendition to your transliteration.
5. **PLAY VIDEO** and **REREAD** written sentence. **HIT PAUSE** button.
6. **PRACTICE INTERPRETING** the sentence using ASL.

Learning Tip *As you practice formulating your interpretation for each sentence, remember to apply rh-questions as addressed in this section.*

7. **PLAY VIDEO** and **VIEW** model. **COMPARE** ASL rendition to your interpretation.
8. **REPEAT** steps 1-7 for each sentence, incorporating the skills you have learned from the models.
9. **REVIEW** the sentences once more to **COMPARE AND CONTRAST** the ASL and PSE renditions of the models for:
   - Word/sign order.
   - Non-manual grammatical features.
   - Vocabulary/sign choices.

Module 4: Rhetorical Questions

4.4 Instructional Activity

"YOU SKILL, HOW (rh-q), PRACTICE!"
10 Minutes

Activity Goal

1. To determine the appropriate ASL lexical item to be used for the rhetorical question in the given examples.

2. To restructure the English sample sentences into appropriate ASL syntax as preparation for interpreting using rhetorical questions.

Activity Instructions

1. REWRITE the following sentences using:

   - The order in which the items would appear if constructed as rhetorical questions.

   - The sign (why, when, what, who, where, for, which, etc.) you would use to indicate the relationship between the two components of the sentence.

Example

| Sentence Order: 1) went store 2) ran out of milk |
| Sign Choice: WHY, FOR FOR, WHAT'S-UP |

I ran out of milk, so I went to the store.

Answer: I went to the store, **why?** I ran out of milk.

Activity Sentences

1. Going to the dentist made me pass out.

2. The baby cried when the dog barked.

3. Many people were angry, so I left quickly.

4. The students were absent because of the flu.

5. All the noise makes her father nervous.

Instructional Guide
©1995 Sign Enhancers, Inc.

4.5 Module Review

"Rh-Questions"
30 Minutes

Activity Goal — To review the information provided within this module by producing each sample sentence using ASL and PSE.

Activity Instructions

1. **REVIEW** section 4.2 Linguistic Information.
2. **REVIEW** the sample sentences from the videotape segment in this section.
3. **READ** each of the English sentences provided in the section below and **APPLY** what you have learned by **PRODUCING** each sentence first using PSE, then ASL.
4. **CHECK** your work by referring to the glosses provided in the following section.

Learning Tip — *It is recommended that you videotape your work. Compare your signed renditions to that of the models on the videotape.*

Activity Sentences

1. My mother lives in Arizona.
2. My father is 68 years old.
3. That man earns one million dollars!
4. I live on a boat.
5. Imagine, my husband got home at two in the morning!
6. Blue is my favorite color.
7. I work at the bank.
8. The boy is 6 feet 4 inches tall!
9. I saw the beautiful flowers on your table.
10. I was just hired because I have 15 years work experience.
11. I found the remote control in the bathroom!
12. I like books that have an inspiring love story.

Module 4: Rhetorical Questions

Comparative Translations

1. *English Sentence:* My mother lives in Arizona.
   PSE Gloss: MY MOTHER LIVE THERE (rt), ARIZONA
   ASL Gloss: MY MOTHER (t), LIVE WHERE (rh-q), THERE (rt), ARIZONA

2. *English Sentence:* My father is 68 years old.
   PSE Gloss: MY FATHER TRUE 68 YEARS-OLD
   ASL Gloss: MY FATHER (t), OLD (rh-q), 68

3. *English Sentence:* That man earns one million dollars!
   PSE Gloss: THAT MAN (rt), EARNS ONE MILLION DOLLARS
   ASL Gloss: THAT MAN (rt) EARNS HOW-MUCH (rh-q), ONE MILLION DOLLARS

4. *English Sentence:* I live on a boat.
   PSE Gloss: ME LIVE THERE (rt) BOAT
   ASL Gloss: ME LIVE WHERE (rh-q), THERE (rt) BOAT

5. *English Sentence:* Imagine, my husband got home at two in the morning!
   PSE Gloss: IMAGINE, MY HUSBAND ARRIVE, TIME 2 MORNING
   ASL Gloss: NERVY, MY HUSBAND ARRIVE, TIME (rh-q), 2 MORNING

6. *English Sentence:* Blue is my favorite color.
   PSE Gloss: BLUE MY FAVORITE COLOR
   ASL Gloss: COLOR ME LIKE (KISS-FIST) (rh-q), BLUE

7. *English Sentence:* I work at the bank.
   PSE Gloss: ME WORK THERE (rt) B-A-N-K
   ASL Gloss: ME WORK WHERE (rh-q), THERE (rt) B-A-N-K

8. *English Sentence:* The boy is 6' 4" tall!
   PSE Gloss: THERE (rt) BOY, 6'4" tall
   ASL Gloss: THERE (rt) BOY (t), TALL WHAT (rh-q), 6'4"

Module 4: Rhetorical Questions

9. *English Sentence:* I saw the beautiful flowers on your table.
   PSE Gloss: I SAW MOST BEAUTIFUL FLOWERS ON YOUR TABLE THERE (rt)
   ASL Gloss: FLOWERS, BEAUTIFUL, ME SAW WHERE (rh-q), YOUR TABLE,(CL:A)(rt),BEAUTIFUL

10. *English Sentence:* I was just hired because I have 15 years of work experience.
    PSE Gloss: ME RECENT HIRE BECAUSE ME HAVE 15 YEARS WORK EXPERIENCE
    ASL Gloss: ME HIRE, WHY (rh-q), ME 15 YEARS ALL-TOGETHER EXPERIENCE WORK

11. *English Sentence:* I found the remote control in the bathroom!
    PSE Gloss: ME FIND TV REMOTE-CONTROL THERE-(rt) BATHROOM
    ASL Gloss: TV REMOTE-CONTROL (t), ME FIND WHERE (rh-q), THERE (rt) BATHROOM

12. *English Sentence:* I like books that have an inspiring love story.
    PSE Gloss: ME LIKE BOOKS THAT HAVE INSPIRE LOVE STORY
    ASL Gloss: BOOKS, ME LIKE (CRAZY-ABOUT) WHAT (rh-q), HAVE LOVE INVOLVED, EFFECT-INSPIRE, LIKE (KISS-FIST)

Module 4: Rhetorical Questions

4.6 Skills Application

"Rh-Questions"
15 Minutes

Activity Goal To practice applying the rh-question format to new stimuli.

Activity Instructions
1. **PRACTICE** applying the information and skills you have learned in this module by **INTERPRETING** the following sentences **USING** rhetorical questions.
2. **APPLY** the non-manual markers associated with producing an ASL sentence using rhetorical questions.
3. **PRACTICE** transliterating each sentence. **COMPARE** the grammatical structure and non-manual markers to your ASL interpretations.

Learning Tips
1. *You can record these sentences onto an audiotape to more closely simulate a voice-to-sign interpreting situation.*
2. *It is recommended that you videotape your work.*

Activity Sentences
1. I want to go to the play because it will be fun.
2. Tom was laughing because I fell.
3. I am going to school to learn ASL.
4. She went to the store to buy toilet paper.
5. Mark bought a new puppy at the pet store.
6. I am going to the bank to deposit some money.
7. ASL is difficult because English is my first language.
8. Shelly wakes up at five o'clock every morning.
9. You should practice the piano so you will improve.
10. You win a race by running fast.

Congratulations!
You have completed Module Four!

5.1 Mini-Lecture
10 Minutes

Activity Goal To comprehend the signed lecture and to identify the main characteristics pertaining to directionality.

Activity Instructions

1. **VIEW** the mini-lecture provided by Nathie Marbury <u>without</u> sound or closed captions.

2. **SUMMARIZE** the mini-lecture in the space allotted below.

3. **CHECK** your understanding by **REPLAYING** the segment, this time with the sound/captions turned on (optional).

Mini-Lecture Summary

_____
_____
_____
_____
_____
_____
_____
_____
_____
_____

Module 5: Directionality

5.2 Linguistic Information

5 Minutes

Activity Goal To provide the learner with a knowledge base that supports the learning experience.

Activity Instructions
1. **READ** the following information pertaining to directionality.
2. **NOTE** any new information.

Linguistic Topic Directionality

In ASL, the movement of some verbs indicates where the action is coming from and where it is going. These verbs are called "directional verbs."

Some examples of verbs whose movements and orientation provide information about the action include:

GIVE	GO
BORROW	COME
SHOW	TELL
LOOK	ASK
WATCH	TEACH

Some examples illustrating these directional verbs are:

1. I-GIVE-TO-YOU
   YOU-GIVE-TO-ME
   HE-GIVE-TO-THEM

2. TOM-BORROW-FROM-YOU
   SHE-BORROW-FROM-HIM
   YOU-BORROW-FROM-ME

3. I-SHOW-YOU
   YOU-SHOW-ME
   SHE-SHOW-US

When using directional verbs, the movement and the orientation of the sign gives you information about who is doing what to whom. But remember, not all ASL verbs are directional!

Module 5: Directionality

5.3 Instructional Activity

"Which Way Did it Go?"
10 Minutes

Activity Goal   To identify English lexical items that can be represented by directional verbs for application in the interpreting and transliterating process.

Activity Instructions

1. **IDENTIFY** and **UNDERLINE** the English words in the sentences below that can be represented by directional verbs.

2. **CHECK** for accuracy by viewing the ASL sample sentences in the videotape segment that corresponds with this module.

Example

The English word(s) that can be represented by a directional verb: GO-TO
I need to go to the store because I ran out of milk.

Activity Sentences

1. Please give your sister a drink.
2. I need help because my car broke down.
3. Do you want to go to the movies?
4. Yes, you can borrow my computer.
5. Can I borrow your car?
6. The teacher asked the girl a question.
7. I need to go to the library.
8. Would you mind helping me clean the house?
9. Give me your keys now!

Instructional Guide
©1995 Sign Enhancers, Inc.

58

Module 5: Directionality

5.4 Video Practice Activity

"Interpreting & Transliterating Skill Development"
30 Minutes

Activity Goal To practice transliterating using PSE and practice interpreting using ASL while learning from the models presented on the videotape.

Activity Instructions

1. **BEGIN** videotaped segment that demonstrates directionality in the sample sentences.

2. **VIEW** written sentence on the screen, **STOP TAPE** by hitting the pause button.

3. **PRACTICE** transliterating the sentence using PSE.

4. **PLAY VIDEO** and **VIEW** model. **COMPARE** PSE rendition to your transliteration.

5. **PLAY VIDEO** and **REREAD** written sentence. **HIT PAUSE** button.

6. **PRACTICE INTERPRETING** the sentence using ASL.

Learning Tip *As you practice formulating your interpretation for each sentence, remember to apply directionality as addressed in this section.*

7. **PLAY VIDEO** and **VIEW** model. **COMPARE** ASL rendition to your interpretation.

8. **REPEAT** steps 1-7 for each sentence, incorporating the skills you have learned from the models.

9. **REVIEW** the sentences once more to **COMPARE AND CONTRAST** the ASL and PSE renditions of the models for:

   • Word/sign order.
   • Non-manual grammatical features.
   • Vocabulary/sign choices.

Instructional Guide
©1995 Sign Enhancers, Inc.

Module 5: Directionality

5.5 Instructional Activity

"Who Did What to Whom?"
15 Minutes

Activity Goals
1. To identify the directional verbs used in the PSE and ASL sample sentences on the videotape.
2. To apply knowledge and skills about directional verbs in order to produce a directional verb appropriately within a new context.

Activity Instructions

1. VIEW each sample sentence on the videotape in the directionality topic area.
2. DETERMINE the directional verb in each sample.
3. PAUSE the tape and sign the sentence again CHANGING who did what to whom by changing the directional movement of the verb.

Learning Tips
1. *Some examples of verbs whose movements and orientation provide information about the action include:*

GIVE	GO
BORROW	COME
SHOW	TELL
LOOK	ASK
WATCH	TEACH

2. *It is recommended that you videotape your work.*

Example 1

Change the direction of the verb, "HELP"
I need help because my car broke down.
Modification: Do you need help because your car broke down?

Example 2

Change the direction of the verb, "GO-TO"
Do you want to go to the movies?
Modification: Do you want to come to my house?

Instructional Guide
©1995 Sign Enhancers, Inc.

Module 5: Directionality

5.6 Module Review

"Directionality"
30 Minutes

Activity Goal — To review the information provided within this module by producing each sample sentence using ASL and PSE.

Activity Instructions

1. **REVIEW** section 5.2 Linguistic Information.
2. **REVIEW** the sample sentences from the videotape segment.
3. **READ** each of the English sentences provided in the section below and **APPLY** what you have learned by **PRODUCING** each sentence first using PSE, then ASL.
4. **CHECK** your work by referring to the glosses provided in the following section.

Learning Tips — *It is recommended that you videotape your work. Compare your signed renditions to that of the models on the videotape.*

Activity Sentences
1. I need to go to the store because I ran out of milk.
2. Please give your sister a drink.
3. I need help because my car broke down.
4. Do you want to go to the movies?
5. Yes, you can borrow my computer.
6. Can I borrow your car?
7. The teacher asked the girl a question.
8. I need to go to the library.
9. Would you mind helping me clean the house?
10. Give me your keys now!

Comparative Translations

1. *English Sentence:* I need to go to the store because I ran out of milk.
   PSE Gloss: I NEED GO (rt) STORE BECAUSE ME RUN-OUT MILK
   ASL Gloss: MILK (t), RUN-OUT, STORE (t) GO-TO (rt) MUST ME

2. *English Sentence:* Please give your sister a drink.
   PSE Gloss: PLEASE GIVE-TO (rt) YOUR SISTER DRINK
   ASL Gloss: YOUR SISTER (t), DRINK (t), GIVE-TO-HER (rt) PLEASE

Instructional Guide
©1995 Sign Enhancers, Inc.

Module 5: Directionality

3. *English Sentence:* I need help because my car broke down.
   PSE Gloss: ME NEED HELP-ME BECAUSE MY CAR BROKE-DOWN
   ASL Gloss: MY CAR (t), BROKE-DOWN, HELP-ME, NEED

4. *English Sentence:* Do you want to go to the movies?
   PSE Gloss: YOU WANT GO-TO (lft) MOVIE (q)
   ASL Gloss: MOVIE (t), GO-TO (lft), WANT (q)

5. *English Sentence:* Yes, you can borrow my computer.
   PSE Gloss: YES, YOU CAN BORROW MY COMPUTER
   ASL Gloss: YES, MY COMPUTER BORROW (rh-q), CAN

6. *English Sentence:* Can I borrow your car?
   PSE Gloss: CAN ME BORROW YOUR CAR (q)
   ASL Gloss: YOUR CAR (t), BORROW CAN (q)

7. *English Sentence:* The teacher asked the girl a question.
   PSE Gloss: TEACHER ASK GIRL (rt) QUESTION (rt)
   ASL Gloss: GIRL (CL:1) (rt), TEACHER ASK-TO (lft to rt)

8. *English Sentence:* I need to go to the library.
   PSE Gloss: I NEED GO-TO (lft) LIBRARY
   ASL Gloss: LIBRARY (t), GO-THERE (lft), MUST

9. *English Sentence:* Would you mind helping me clean the house?
   PSE Gloss: YOU DON'T-MIND HELP-ME CLEAN HOUSE (q)
   ASL Gloss: HOUSE CLEAN (t), HELP-ME, DON'T-MIND (q)

10. *English Sentence:* Give me your keys now!
    PSE Gloss: GIVE-TO-ME KEYS NOW
    ASL Gloss: KEYS (t), GIVE-TO-ME NOW

Instructional Guide
©1995 Sign Enhancers, Inc.

Module 5: Directionality

5.7 Skills Application

"Directionality"
15 Minutes

Activity Goal — To practice applying directionality to new stimuli.

Activity Instructions
1. **PRACTICE** applying the information and skills you have learned in this module by **INTERPRETING** the following sentences **USING** directionality.
2. **APPLY** the non-manual markers associated with producing an ASL sentence using directionality.
3. **PRACTICE** transliterating each sentence. **COMPARE** the grammatical structure and non-manual markers to your ASL interpretations.

Learning Tip — *You can record these sentences onto an audiotape to more closely simulate a voice-to-sign interpreting situation.*

Activity Sentences
1. The teacher passed out the tests to all the students.
2. Did Mary give you the book?
3. Please pass me the salt.
4. The little girl gave her food to the dog under the table.
5. John borrowed my bike.
6. Will you teach me how to play the piano?
7. I want you to watch me play tennis.
8. I saw the boy hit the girl.
9. Throw the ball to Jerry.
10. Pay close attention to how the teacher signs.

Congratulations!
You have completed Module Five!

Instructional Guide
©1995 Sign Enhancers, Inc.

MODULE 6: Use of Space

6.1 Mini-Lecture
10 Minutes

Activity Goal — To comprehend the signed lecture and to identify the main characteristics involved in the grammatical aspect of use of space.

Activity Instructions

1. **VIEW** the mini-lecture provided by Nathie Marbury <u>without</u> sound or closed captions.
2. **SUMMARIZE** the mini-lecture in the space allotted below.
3. **CHECK** your understanding by **REPLAYING** the segment, this time with the sound/captions turned on (optional).

Mini-Lecture Summary

_____
_____
_____
_____
_____
_____
_____
_____
_____
_____
_____
_____

Module 6: Use of Space

6.2 Linguistic Information
10 Minutes

Activity Goal To provide the learner with a knowledge base that supports the learning experience.

Activity Instructions
1. **READ** the following information pertaining to use of space.
2. **NOTE** any new information.

Linguistic Topic

Use of Space

In ASL, the placement of signs is extremely important. Often, a sign representing a place, person or object is signed in a specific space so that it may be referred to again. This feature of placing people, places and things in a space is one aspect of what is referred to as "use of space."

For example, if a signer were to discuss her mother who was not in the room, she might establish a space for her mom by pointing to the area at the signer's right. The signer might want to introduce her dad in the same context as her mom. In this case, the signer may establish the space to her left as a reference area for her father.

For example:

MY MOM (t), (rt) {placed on the right of the signer by pointing and eye gaze}, WAIT+WAIT

MY DAD (t), (lft) {placed on the left of the signer by pointing and eye gaze}, LATE

SHE (rt), PATIENT

HE (lft), HURRY, TRY+TRY

You can see from this example that the signer's mother is established in the space to her right, and her father is established in the space to her left. Therefore, further references to either person can be made by pointing (or indicating with an eye gaze) to one of these areas. This method of referencing a person or persons who are not actually present utilizes what we call "absent referents" or "indexing."

You will notice when a signer establishes and uses a referent, the eyes usually will gaze in the direction of the referent. This eye gaze is an important cue and can even replace pointing.

Module 6: Use of Space

There are many other use of space features used in ASL. This course will primarily focus on absent referents. However, as you view the sample sentences, see if you can pick out other ways the signing models use spatial features to clarify the message.

6.3 Video Practice Activity

"Interpreting & Transliterating Skill Development"
30 Minutes

Activity Goal To practice transliterating using PSE and practice interpreting using ASL while learning from the models presented on the videotape.

Activity Instructions

1. **BEGIN** videotaped segment that demonstrates use of space in the sample sentences.

2. **VIEW** written sentence on the screen, **STOP TAPE** by hitting the pause button.

3. **PRACTICE** transliterating the sentence using PSE.

4. **PLAY VIDEO** and **VIEW** model. **COMPARE** PSE rendition to your transliteration.

5. **PLAY VIDEO** and **REREAD** written sentence. **HIT PAUSE** button.

6. **PRACTICE INTERPRETING** the sentence using ASL.

Learning Tip *As you practice formulating your interpretation for each sentence, remember to apply use of space features as addressed in this section.*

7. **PLAY VIDEO** and **VIEW** model. **COMPARE** ASL rendition to your interpretation.

8. **REPEAT** steps 1-7 for each sentence, incorporating the skills you have learned from the models.

9. **REVIEW** the sentences once more to **COMPARE AND CONTRAST** the ASL and PSE renditions of the models for:

   - Word/sign order.
   - Non-manual grammatical features.
   - Vocabulary/sign choices.

Module 6: Use of Space

6.4 Instructional Activity

"Venturing into Space"
15 Minutes

Activity Goal To compare how use of space features are used in PSE and ASL.

Activity Instructions

1. **VIEW** each signed sample sentence on the videotape in the use of space section.

2. **DETERMINE** which of the PSE and ASL sentences incorporate use of space features (for example, absent referent, character shifts, comparison and contrast, etc.).

3. **USING** the sentences and check-list below, check in either or both of the PSE and ASL options indicating the fact that use of space features have been used.

Example

This sentence uses an absent referent for "the girl" in both ASL & PSE.	Check if "use of space" is used.
Who is that red-headed girl?	✓ PSE ✓ ASL

Activity Sentences

1. That big yellow house is mine.   ___PSE   ___ASL
2. I have two sons and one daughter.   ___PSE   ___ASL
3. My friend will come to my house to visit.   ___PSE   ___ASL
4. Do you walk or drive to school?   ___PSE   ___ASL
5. Are you married or single?   ___PSE   ___ASL
6. Are you hungry or thirsty?   ___PSE   ___ASL
7. I love my new house in the woods!   ___PSE   ___ASL
8. I need help moving my piano!   ___PSE   ___ASL

Instructional Guide
©1995 Sign Enhancers, Inc.

Module 6: Use of Space

9. Do you want to drive to the store together?	___PSE	___ASL
10. Bob looks like his father.	___PSE	___ASL
11. I am named after my grandfather's sister.	___PSE	___ASL

6.5 Module Review

"Use of Space"
30 Minutes

Activity Goal — To review the information provided within this module by producing each sample sentence using ASL and PSE.

Activity Instructions

1. **REVIEW** section 6.2 Linguistic Information.
2. **REVIEW** the sample sentences from the videotape segment in this section.
3. **READ** each of the English sentences provided in the section below and **APPLY** what you have learned by **PRODUCING** each sentence first using PSE, then ASL.
4. **CHECK** your work by referring to the glosses provided in the following section.

Learning Tips — *It is recommended that you videotape your work. Compare your signed renditions to that of the models on the videotape.*

Activity Sentences

1. Who is that red-headed girl?
2. That big yellow house is mine.
3. I have two sons and one daughter.
4. My friend will come to my house to visit.
5. Do you walk or drive to school?
6. Are you married or single?
7. Are you hungry or thirsty?
8. I love my new house in the woods!
9. I need help moving my piano.
10. Do you want to drive to the store together?
11. Bob looks like his father.
12. I am named after my grandfather's sister.

Module 6: Use of Space

Comparative Translations

1. *English Sentence:* Who is that red-headed girl?
   PSE Gloss: WHO (wh-q) THAT (rt) RED+HAIR GIRL
   ASL Gloss: THAT GIRL, THERE (rt) RED+HAIR (t), WHO (wh-q)

2. *English Sentence:* That big yellow house is mine.
   PSE Gloss: THAT (lft) BIG, YELLOW HOUSE, MINE
   ASL Gloss: THAT BIG, YELLOW, HOUSE (lft) (t), MINE

3. *English Sentence:* I have two sons and one daughter.
   PSE Gloss: ME HAVE TWO SON (lft) + SON (lft), ONE DAUGHTER (rt)
   ASL Gloss: SON+SON, TWO (lft), DAUGHTER, ONE (rt), HAVE ME

4. *English Sentence:* My friend will come to my house to visit.
   PSE Gloss: MY FRIEND WILL COME-TO MY HOUSE VISIT
   ASL Gloss: MY FRIEND (lft) (t), MY HOUSE (rt) (t), COME (lft to rt) VISIT WILL

5. *English Sentence:* Do you walk or drive to school?
   PSE Gloss: YOU WALK (lft) O-R DRIVE-TO (rt) SCHOOL (wh-q)
   ASL Gloss: SCHOOL ARRIVE HOW(rh-q), WALK (lft), DRIVE (rt), WHICH (wh-q)

6. *English Sentence:* Are you married or single?
   PSE Gloss: YOU MARRY O-R SINGLE (wh-q)
   ASL Gloss: YOU MARRY (lft), SINGLE (rt), WHICH (wh-q)

7. *English Sentence:* Are you hungry or thirsty?
   PSE Gloss: YOU HUNGRY (rt), THIRSTY (lft) (wh-q)
   ASL Gloss: HUNGRY (rt), THIRSTY (lft), WHICH (wh-q)

Instructional Guide
©1995 Sign Enhancers, Inc.

8. *English Sentence:* I love my new house in the woods!

   PSE Gloss: I LOVE MY NEW HOUSE, WOODS

   ASL Gloss: MY NEW HOUSE (CL:A), WOODS, ME LOVE (KISS-FIST)

9. *English Sentence:* I need help moving my piano.

   PSE Gloss: I NEED HELP-ME MOVE MY PIANO

   ASL Gloss: MY PIANO (t), MOVE (to left), (mime-moving piano) HELP-ME, NEED

10. *English Sentence:* Do you want to drive to the store together?

    PSE Gloss: YOU WANT DRIVE-TO STORE TOGETHER (q)

    ASL Gloss: STORE (t), TWO-OF-US GET-IN-CAR, DRIVE-TO-STORE (lft) (q)

11. *English Sentence:* Bob looks like his father.

    PSE Gloss: BOB (lft) LOOKS-SAME HIS (lft) FATHER (rt)

    ASL Gloss: BOB (lft), HIS FATHER (rt) HE (lft) LOOK STRONG SAME-AS HE (rt)

12. *English Sentence:* I am named after my grandfather's sister.

    PSE Gloss: ME NAME FOR MY GRANDFATHER (rt), HIS (rt) SISTER

    ASL Gloss: MY NAME, HOW HAPPEN (rh-q), MY GRANDFATHER (rt), HIS SISTER (lft), HONOR-HER (lft)

Module 6: Use of Space

6.6 Skills Application

"Use of Space"
15 Minutes

Activity Goal — To practice applying use of space features to new stimuli.

Activity Instructions
1. **PRACTICE** applying the information and skills you have learned in this module by **INTERPRETING** the following sentences **USING** use of space features.
2. **APPLY** the non-manual markers associated with producing an ASL sentence with use of space features.
3. **PRACTICE** transliterating each sentence. **COMPARE** the grammatical structure and non-manual markers to your ASL interpretations.

Learning Tips
1. *You can record these sentences onto an audiotape to more closely simulate a voice-to-sign interpreting situation.*
2. *It is recommended that you videotape your work.*

Activity Sentences
1. Jack is moving to Oregon next week.
2. You need to drive up a steep hill to get to my house.
3. The little girl got scared when the big dog approached her.
4. That woman owns and runs six companies.
5. Jane and Bob ran to each other and kissed for a long time.
6. Is your house in the city or in the country?
7. Mom gave Dad a stern look.
8. Who is that man with the black coat?
9. That big motorcycle belongs to my sister.
10. For my vacation, I am driving all the way from Washington state to southern California.

Congratulations!
You have completed Module Six!

MODULE 7: Negation

7.1 Mini-Lecture
10 Minutes

Activity Goal To comprehend the signed lecture and to identify the main characteristics involved in producing sentences using negation.

Activity Instructions
1. **VIEW** the mini-lecture provided by Nathie Marbury <u>without</u> sound or closed captions.
2. **SUMMARIZE** the mini-lecture in the space allotted below.
3. **CHECK** your understanding by **REPLAYING** the segment, this time with the sound/captions turned on (optional).

Mini-Lecture Summary

_____
_____
_____
_____
_____
_____
_____
_____
_____
_____
_____
_____

Module 7: Negation

7.2 Linguistic Information
10 Minutes

Activity Goal To provide the learner with a knowledge base that supports the learning experience.

Activity Instructions
1. **READ** the following information pertaining to negation.
2. **NOTE** any new information.

Linguistic Topic

Negation

Negation as shown in ASL is almost always accompanied by a negative headshake. The placement of the sign indicating the negative is most often placed at the end of the sentence, or following the verb or adjective it negates.

Examples of some common vocabulary used to present a negative include:
- NOT
- DON'T
- NO
- CAN'T
- WON'T

Examples of comparative sentences demonstrating the difference in placement of negation between English and ASL are:

Example 1
English: I am not happy.
ASL: HAPPY, NOT (me)

Example 2
English: I can't find my money.
ASL: MY MONEY (t), FIND, CAN'T (me)

Example 3
English: Don't hit your brother!
ASL: YOUR BROTHER (t), HIT-HIM, DON'T (you)

NOTE: In each of the examples above, the signs indicating negation (NOT, CAN'T, DON'T) are actually not necessary if a negative headshake is simultaneously produced with the sentence.

Instructional Guide
©1995 Sign Enhancers, Inc.

7.3 Video Practice Activity

"Interpreting & Transliterating Skill Development"
30 Minutes

Activity Goal To practice transliterating using PSE and practice interpreting using ASL while learning from the models presented on the videotape.

Activity Instructions

1. **BEGIN** videotaped segment that demonstrates negation in the sample sentences.

2. **VIEW** written sentence on the screen, **STOP TAPE** by hitting the pause button.

3. **PRACTICE** transliterating the sentence using PSE.

4. **PLAY VIDEO** and **VIEW** model. **COMPARE** PSE rendition to your transliteration.

5. **PLAY VIDEO** and **REREAD** written sentence. **HIT PAUSE** button.

6. **PRACTICE INTERPRETING** the sentence using ASL.

Learning Tip *As you practice formulating your interpretation for each sentence, remember to apply negation as addressed in this section.*

7. **PLAY VIDEO** and **VIEW** model. **COMPARE** ASL rendition to your interpretation.

8. **REPEAT** steps 1-7 for each sentence, incorporating the skills you have learned from the models.

9. **REVIEW** the sentences once more to **COMPARE AND CONTRAST** the ASL and PSE renditions of the models for:

   - Word/sign order.
   - Non-manual grammatical features.
   - Vocabulary/sign choices.

Module 7: Negation

7.4 Instructional Activity

"Don't Be So Negative!"
15 Minutes

Activity Goal To distinguish between a negative and a positive statement, and to accurately produce the linguistic features that accompany each.

Activity Instructions

1. **VIEW** each sample sentence in the negation topic area.
2. **PAUSE** the tape and **REPRODUCE** each sample sentence until you are confident you are reproducing it accurately.
3. **SIGN** the sentence again, this time **CHANGE** it into a positive statement.

Example

English/negative:	I don't have any children.
PSE/negative:	_____ neg. headshake ME NOT HAVE CHILDREN
English/positive:	I have children.
PSE/positive:	_____ pos. headnod ME HAVE CHILDREN
ASL/negative:	_____ neg headshake CHILDREN (t), HAVE NONE (me)
ASL/positive:	_____ pos. headnod CHILDREN (t), HAVE (me)

Instructional Guide
©1995 Sign Enhancers, Inc.

7.5 Module Review

"Negation"
30 Minutes

Activity Goal To review the information provided within this module by producing each sample sentence using ASL and PSE.

Activity Instructions

1. **REVIEW** section 7.2 Linguistic Information of this module.
2. **REVIEW** the sample sentences from the video segment in this section.
3. **READ** each of the English sentences provided in the section below and **APPLY** what you have learned by **PRODUCING** each sentence first using PSE, then ASL.
4. **CHECK** your work by referring to the glosses provided in the following section.

Learning Tip *It is recommended that you videotape your work. Compare your signed renditions to that of the models on the video.*

Activity Sentences
1. I don't have any children.
2. I'm not going to the library today.
3. Don't hit your sister!
4. I can't find my glasses!
5. I am not happy.
6. Why can't I go to the store?
7. I don't understand that math problem!
8. I don't want to go to work.
9. I can't read your fingerspelling.
10. Tom didn't like my picture.

Comparative Translations
1. *English Sentence:* I don't have any children.
   PSE Gloss: ME NOT HAVE ANY CHILDREN
   ASL Gloss: CHILDREN (t), HAVE NONE, ME

Module 7: Negation

2. *English Sentence:* I am not going to the library today.
   PSE Gloss: ME NOT GO-TO (lft) LIBRARY TODAY
   ASL Gloss: TODAY, LIBRARY (t), GO-TO (lft), NOT

3. *English Sentence:* Don't hit your sister!
   PSE Gloss: DON'T HIT (lft) YOUR SISTER
   ASL Gloss: YOUR SISTER (lft) (t), HIT-HER (lft), DON'T

4. *English Sentence:* I can't find my glasses!
   PSE Gloss: ME CAN'T FIND MY GLASSES
   ASL Gloss: MY GLASSES FIND, CAN'T

5. *English Sentence:* I am not happy.
   PSE Gloss: ME NOT HAPPY
   ASL Gloss: ME HAPPY , NOT

6. *English Sentence:* Why can't I go to the store?
   PSE Gloss: WHY CAN'T ME GO-TO (rt) STORE (wh-q)
   ASL Gloss: STORE (t), GO-TO (rt), CAN'T, WHY-NOT (wh-q)

7. *English Sentence:* I don't understand that math problem!
   PSE Gloss: ME NOT UNDERSTAND THAT (rt) MATH PROBLEM
   ASL Gloss: THAT (rt) PROBLEM, MATH (t), ME UNDERSTAND, NOT

8. *English Sentence:* I don't want to go to work!
   PSE Gloss: ME DON'T-WANT GO-TO (rt) WORK
   ASL Gloss: WORK GO-THERE (rt), DON'T-WANT

9. *English Sentence:* I can't read your fingerspelling.
   PSE Gloss: ME CAN'T READ YOUR FINGERSPELLING
   ASL Gloss: YOU FINGERSPELL-TO-ME, UNDERSTAND, CAN'T

10. *English Sentence:* Tom didn't like my picture.
    PSE Gloss: TOM NOT-LIKE MY PICTURE
    ASL Gloss: MY PICTURE (t), TOM NOT-LIKE

Module 7: Negation

7.6 Skills Application

"Negation"
15 Minutes

Activity Goal To practice applying negation to new stimuli.

Activity Instructions
1. **PRACTICE** applying the information and skills you have learned in this module by **INTERPRETING** the following sentences using negation.
2. **APPLY** the non-manual markers associated with producing an ASL sentence using negation.
3. **PRACTICE** transliterating each sentence. **COMPARE** the grammatical structure and non-manual markers to your ASL interpretations.

Learning Tips
1. *You can record these sentences onto an audiotape to more closely simulate a voice-to-sign interpreting situation.*
2. *It is recommended that you videotape your work.*

Activity Sentences
1. I did not like that movie.
2. Betty was not interested in Bob at all.
3. There isn't any milk left.
4. Jerry doesn't have your phone number.
5. The cat wasn't hungry.
6. Bill doesn't know any Sign Language.
7. Not one of those students passed the course.
8. I didn't understand that book at all!
9. Mark didn't get the job.
10. I don't have any money.

Congratulations!
You have completed Module Seven!

MODULE 8 — Classifiers

8.1 Mini-Lecture
15 Minutes

Activity Goal — To comprehend the signed lecture and to identify the main characteristics involved in using classifiers.

Activity Instructions

1. **VIEW** the mini-lecture provided by Nathie Marbury <u>without</u> sound or closed captions.

2. **SUMMARIZE** the mini-lecture in the space allotted below.

3. **CHECK** your understanding by **REPLAYING** the segment, this time with the sound/captions turned on (optional).

Mini-Lecture Summary

_____
_____
_____
_____
_____
_____
_____
_____
_____
_____
_____

Module 8: Classifiers

8.2 Linguistic Information
10 Minutes

Activity Goal — To provide the learner with a knowledge base that supports the learning experience.

Activity Instructions
1. **READ** the following information pertaining to the use of classifiers.
2. **NOTE** any new information.

Linguistic Topic

Classifiers

Classifiers are a type of sign that represent a "class" of objects. They are used in ASL to describe the movement, placement, and visual characteristics of a person or object.

For example, a classifier composed of the thumb, index and middle fingers (CL:3) can represent a number of vehicles (that all have wheels and basically move the same way):

- CAR
- BUS
- BICYCLE
- TRUCK
- TRAIN

However, vehicles that move differently, such as an airplane, skateboard, sled, etc. would not be accurately represented by this particular classifier.

Once an object is identified, a classifier can be used to show how that object moves and its relationship to other objects.

The following are some examples of classifiers and the groupings of objects they represent:

- CL:3 (thumb, index and middle fingers) = Certain vehicles

- CL:1 (index finger) = Upright person or thin cylinder shaped objects such as a pencil, cigarette, pole, etc.

- CL:Bent V (index and middle finger curved) = A person or some animals in sitting position

- CL:A ("A" handshape) = Establishment of an object in space, such as a house, statue, computer, etc.

- CL:C ("C" handshape) = A cup, cylinder, pole, thick rope, pipe, etc.

Module 8: Classifiers

Note: Classifiers are used frequently because they enable easy manipulation of signs in space. The examples of classifiers presented in this lesson are but a few of those actually used within ASL. As you are exposed to more ASL linguistic samples, the importance of classifiers will become evident.

8.3 Instructional Activity

"In a Class of Their Own!"
15 Minutes

Activity Goal To identify which components of each English sentence are represented by classifiers on the videotape.

Activity Instructions

1. **VIEW** each sentence on the videotape in the classifier topic area.

2. On the script below **UNDERLINE** the concepts which are represented by a classifier as signed by the model.

Learning Tip *Be sure to notice the classifier and the information provided by the movement of the classifier.*

Example

CL:1 is used to show the man and how he moved in space.
The <u>man walked as if he were drunk</u>.

Activity Sentences
1. The horse ran very fast!
2. The students lined up at the door.
3. The students sat in a semicircle with the teacher in the middle.
4. The man sat near the tree.
5. The cows were all grazing in the field.
6. The boy gets to school on a horse.
7. The car drove right into the house.
8. There were so many people at the show last night.

8.4 Video Practice Activity

"Interpreting & Transliterating Skill Development"
30 Minutes

Activity Goal To practice transliterating using PSE and practice interpreting using ASL while learning from the models presented on the videotape.

Activity Instructions

1. **BEGIN** videotaped segment that demonstrates classifiers in the sample sentences.

2. **VIEW** written sentence on the screen, **STOP TAPE** by hitting the pause button.

3. **PRACTICE** transliterating the sentence using PSE.

4. **PLAY VIDEO** and **VIEW** model. **COMPARE** PSE rendition to your transliteration.

5. **PLAY VIDEO** and **REREAD** written sentence. **HIT PAUSE** button.

6. **PRACTICE INTERPRETING** the sentence using ASL.

Learning Tip *As you practice formulating your interpretation for each sentence, remember to apply classifiers as addressed in this section.*

7. **PLAY VIDEO** and **VIEW** model. **COMPARE** ASL rendition to your interpretation.

8. **REPEAT** steps 1-7 for each sentence, incorporating the skills you have learned from the models.

9. **REVIEW** the sentences once more to **COMPARE AND CONTRAST** the ASL and PSE renditions of the models for:

   - Word/sign order.
   - Non-manual grammatical features.
   - Vocabulary/sign choices.

8.5 Instructional Activity

"Have You Seen Any Good Classifiers Lately?"
15 Minutes

Activity Goal To compare the use of classifiers in PSE and ASL.

Activity Instructions
1. **VIEW** each sample sentence on the videotape in the classifiers topic area.
2. **NOTE** and **COMPARE** the classifiers and sign vocabulary used in the PSE and ASL renditions.

Example

A CL:1 classifier was used in the ASL version.	Check if classifiers are used:
The man walked as if he were drunk.	___PSE ✔ ASL

Activity Sentences

1. The horse ran very fast!   ___PSE ___ASL
2. The students lined up at the door.   ___PSE ___ASL
3. The students sat in a semicircle with the teacher in the middle.   ___PSE ___ASL
4. The man sat near the tree.   ___PSE ___ASL
5. The cows were all grazing in the field.   ___PSE ___ASL
6. The boy gets to school on a horse.   ___PSE ___ASL
7. The car drove right into the house.   ___PSE ___ASL
8. There were so many people at the show last night.   ___PSE ___ASL

Module 8: Classifiers

8.6 Module Review

"Classifiers"
30 Minutes

Activity Goal To review the information provided within this module by producing each sample sentence using ASL and PSE.

Activity Instructions

1. **REVIEW** section 8.2 Linguistic Information of this module.

2. **REVIEW** the sample sentences from the video segment in this section.

3. **READ** each of the English sentences provided in the section below and **APPLY** what you have learned by **PRODUCING** each sentence first using PSE, then ASL.

4. **CHECK** your work by referring to the glosses provided in the following section.

Learning Tip *It is recommended that you videotape your work. Compare your signed renditions to that of the models on the video.*

Activity Sentences

1. The man walked as if he were drunk.
2. The horse ran very fast!
3. The students lined up at the door.
4. The students sat in a semicircle with the teacher in the middle.
5. The man sat near the tree.
6. The cows were all grazing in the field.
7. The boy gets to school on a horse.
8. The car drove right into the house.
9. There were so many people at the show last night.

Comparative Translations

1. *English Sentence:* The man walked as if he were drunk.
   PSE Gloss: THERE (rt) MAN WALKED, LOOK-LIKE DRUNK
   ASL Gloss: MAN THERE (rt) (t), WALK (CL:1) LOOK-LIKE DRUNK

Module 8: Classifiers

2. *English Sentence:* The horse ran very fast!
   PSE Gloss: HORSE RUN+RUN+RUN+RUN, FAST
   ASL Gloss: HORSE (t), RUN+RUN+RUN+RUN, ZOOM-AWAY (lft)

3. *English Sentence:* The students lined up at the door.
   PSE Gloss: STUDENT, LINE-UP DOOR THERE (lft)
   ASL Gloss: DOOR (t), STUDENT (t), LINE-UP

4. *English Sentence:* The students sat in a semicircle with teacher in the middle.
   PSE Gloss: STUDENT+STUDENT, SIT (CL: Bent V) WITH TEACHER SIT MIDDLE
   ASL Gloss: TEACHER (t), SIT, STUDENT+STUDENT (t) (CL: Bent V), (AROUND TEACHER)

5. *English Sentence:* The man sat near the tree.
   PSE Gloss: MAN SIT NEAR TREE
   ASL Gloss: TREE (t), MAN, SIT-NEAR (CL: Bent V)

6. *English Sentence:* The cows were all grazing in the field.
   PSE Gloss: COWS A-L-L CHEWING THERE (rt) FIELD (GRASS+LAND)
   ASL Gloss: FIELD (GRASS+LAND), COWS (t), (CL: Bent V) (lft, rt, lft) A-L-L CHEWING (lft, rt, lft)

7. *English Sentence:* The boy gets to school on a horse.
   PSE Gloss: BOY ARRIVE (rt) SCHOOL, HORSE-RIDE
   ASL Gloss: BOY ARRIVE (rt) SCHOOL, HOW (rh-q), HORSE-RIDE

8. *English Sentence:* The car drove right into the house.
   PSE Gloss: CAR DRIVE CRASH-INTO (lft) HOUSE
   ASL Gloss: HOUSE (CL:A) (lft), CAR, (CL:3) DRIVE-INTO-HOUSE

Instructional Guide
©1995 Sign Enhancers, Inc.

Module 8: Classifiers

9.	*English Sentence:*	There were so many people at the show last night.
	PSE Gloss:	TRUE MANY PEOPLE THERE (rt) PLAY, LAST NIGHT
	ASL Gloss:	LAST NIGHT, PLAY (rt), (CL:Bent 5)

8.7 Skills Application

"Classifiers"
15 Minutes

Activity Goal To practice applying classifiers to new stimuli.

Activity Instructions

1. **PRACTICE** applying the information and skills you have learned in this module by **INTERPRETING** the following sentences using classifiers.

2. **PRACTICE** transliterating each sentence. **COMPARE** the grammatical structure and non-manual markers to your ASL interpretations.

Learning Tips

1. *You can record these sentences onto an audiotape to more closely simulate a voice-to-sign interpreting situation.*

2. *It is recommended that you videotape your work.*

Activity Sentences

1. The children sat down on the floor in a circle.
2. The horse just stood in the rain.
3. The dog jumped up and down when Joe got home.
4. The huge old tree fell down in the storm.
5. Please line up behind the computer now.
6. The bus skid in the snow.
7. Eileen put her award on the shelf.
8. The cars raced each other down the dirt road.
9. The little boy fell off the bike.
10. Sue missed the bus so she rode her horse to school.

Congratulations!
You have completed Module Eight!

Module 9: Conditionals

MODULE 9: Conditional Sentence Types

9.1 Mini-Lecture
10 Minutes

Activity Goal To comprehend the signed lecture and to identify the main characteristics involved in producing conditionals.

Activity Instructions

1. **VIEW** the mini-lecture provided by Nathie Marbury <u>without</u> sound or closed captions.

2. **SUMMARIZE** the mini-lecture in the space allotted below.

3. **CHECK** your understanding by **REPLAYING** the segment, this time with the sound/captions turned on (optional).

Mini-Lecture Summary

_____

_____

_____

_____

_____

_____

_____

_____

_____

_____

_____

Module 9: Conditionals

9.2 Linguistic Information
10 Minutes

Activity Goal   To provide the learner with a knowledge base that supports the learning experience.

Activity Instructions
1. **READ** the following information pertaining to the use of conditionals.
2. **NOTE** any new information.

Linguistic Topic

Conditionals

In ASL, when there is a causal relationship between two portions of a signed discourse such that **if** one thing occurs, **then** something else would happen, the structure used is called a "conditional."

For example:

- If it rains, the ball game will be canceled.
- If I get a 'D' on the test, Dad will get mad.
- If you understand how to recognize conditionals, we will be pleased.

You can see from the examples above that there are two components to a conditional. The "IF" or "SUPPOSE" portion of the sentence is the first. This portion is established with the following non-manual grammatical markers:

- Brow raise.
- Slight head tilt.
- Hold last sign of condition.

The condition is often introduced using the signs, I-F or SUPPOSE, but the use of the above grammatical markers in conjunction with the signs explaining the condition actually make these signs unnecessary.

The second portion of the conditional statement, the consequence or the "THEN" portion is indicated with the following grammatical markers:

- The head returns to an upright position from the "slight head tilt."
- The head often nods affirmatively.

Remember when producing a conditional sentence type, the condition usually precedes the consequence.

Instructional Guide
©*1995 Sign Enhancers, Inc.*

9.3 Instructional Activity

"If Only..."
5 Minutes

Activity Goal To identify the two main components of the conditional ("if" and "then") within the English sentences provided below.

Activity Instructions

1. **READ** the following sentences to **DETERMINE** the "if" and "then" conditional grammatical features within each sentence.

2. **IDENTIFY** the "if" feature contained in the sentence by **CIRCLING** the entire condition ("if") clause.

3. **IDENTIFY** the "then" feature contained in the sentence by **UNDERLINING** the consequence ("then") clause.

4. **CHECK** for accuracy by viewing the ASL conditional sample sentences on the videotape.

Example

> <u>If</u> you wash my car, <u>**then**</u> I'll teach you Sign Language.
>
> <u>I'll teach you Sign Language</u> in exchange for (washing my car.)

Activity Sentences

1. My mom will be proud if I get an "A" on that test.

2. I will be broke if I buy that shirt.

3. The chair may break if you sit on it.

4. My boss will fire me if I call in sick again.

5. That little boy will cry if you don't give him a bottle.

Module 9: Conditionals

9.4 Video Practice Activity

"Interpreting & Transliterating Skill Development"
30 Minutes

Activity Goal To practice transliterating using PSE and practice interpreting using ASL while learning from the models presented on the videotape.

Activity Instructions

1. **BEGIN** videotaped segment that demonstrates conditionals in the sample sentences.

2. **VIEW** written sentence on the screen, **STOP TAPE** by hitting the pause button.

3. **PRACTICE** transliterating the sentence using PSE.

4. **PLAY VIDEO** and **VIEW** model. **COMPARE** PSE rendition to your transliteration.

5. **PLAY VIDEO** and **REREAD** written sentence. **HIT PAUSE** button.

6. **PRACTICE INTERPRETING** the sentence using ASL.

Learning Tip *As you practice formulating your interpretation for each sentence, remember to apply conditionals as addressed in this section.*

7. **PLAY VIDEO** and **VIEW** model. **COMPARE** ASL rendition to your interpretation.

8. **REPEAT** steps 1-7 for each sentence, incorporating the skills you have learned from the models.

9. **REVIEW** the sentences once more to **COMPARE AND CONTRAST** the ASL and PSE renditions of the models for:

- Word/sign order.
- Non-manual grammatical features.
- Vocabulary/sign choices.

Module 9: Conditionals

9.5 Module Review

"Conditionals"
30 Minutes

Activity Goal To review the information provided within this module by producing each sample sentence using ASL and PSE.

Activity Instructions

1. **REVIEW** section 9.2 Linguistic Information of this module.
2. **REVIEW** the sample sentences from the video segment in this section.
3. **READ** each of the English sentences provided in the section below and **APPLY** what you have learned by **PRODUCING** each sentence first using PSE, then ASL.
4. **CHECK** your work by referring to the glosses provided in the following section.

Learning Tip *It is recommended that you videotape your work. Compare your signed renditions to that of the models on the video.*

Activity Sentences

1. I'll teach you Sign Language in exchange for washing my car.
2. My mom will be proud if I get an "A" on that test.
3. I will be broke if I buy that shirt.
4. The chair may break if you sit on it.
5. My boss will fire me if I call in sick again.
6. That little boy will cry if you don't give him a bottle.

Comparative Translations

1. *English Sentence:* I'll teach you Sign Language in exchange for washing my car.
   PSE Gloss: ME WILL TEACH YOU SIGN LANGUAGE SUBSTITUTE YOU WASH CAR
   ASL Gloss: SIGN LANGUAGE (t), ME TEACH-TO-YOU, DON'T-MIND... UNDERSTAND (cond), MY CAR (t), YOU WASH, EXCHANGE

Instructional Guide
©1995 Sign Enhancers, Inc.

Module 9: Conditionals

2. *English Sentence:* My mom will be proud if I get an "A" on that test.
   PSE Gloss: MY MOM WILL PROUD I-F ME GET "A" TEST
   ASL Gloss: IF ME TEST, "A" (cond), MOM, PROUD WILL SHE (rt)

3. *English Sentence:* I will be broke if I buy that shirt.
   PSE Gloss: ME WILL BROKE I-F ME BUY THAT (rt) SHIRT
   ASL Gloss: SUPPOSE THAT (rt) SHIRT, ME BUY (cond), BROKE ME, WILL

4. *English Sentence:* The chair may break if you sit on it.
   PSE Gloss: THIS CHAIR (rt) MAYBE BREAK I-F YOU SIT-THERE (rt)
   ASL Gloss: CHAIR, THERE (rt) (t), SUPPOSE YOU SIT-THERE (rt) (cond), BREAK-DOWN, WILL

5. *English Sentence:* My boss will fire me if I call in sick again.
   PSE Gloss: MY BOSS WILL FIRE ME I-F ME CALL-TO-BOSS SICK AGAIN
   ASL Gloss: SUPPOSE ME CALL-TO-BOSS (rt), SICK AGAIN (cond), WHAT (rh-q), FIRE-ME, WILL

6. *English Sentence:* That little boy will cry if you don't give him a bottle.
   PSE Gloss: LITTLE BOY (rt) WILL CRY+CRY I-F YOU NOT GIVE-TO (rt) BOTTLE
   ASL Gloss: BOY, LITTLE (rt) (t), SUPPOSE BOTTLE, GIVE-HIM, REFUSE (cond), CRY+CRY+CRY WILL HE (rt)

Module 9: Conditionals

9.6 Skills Application

"Conditionals"
15 Minutes

Activity Goal   To practice applying conditionals to new stimuli.

Activity Instructions

1. **PRACTICE** applying the information and skills you have learned in this module by **INTERPRETING** the following sentences using conditionals.

2. **APPLY** the non-manual markers associated with producing an ASL sentence using conditionals.

3. **PRACTICE** transliterating each sentence. **COMPARE** the grammatical structure and non-manual markers to your ASL interpretations.

Learning Tips

1. *You can record these sentences onto an audiotape to more closely simulate a voice-to-sign interpreting situation.*

2. *It is recommended that you videotape your work.*

Activity Sentences

1. You can have dessert if you eat your beans.
2. Hard work is required for success.
3. I'll watch your house if I can use your computer.
4. I'm not going to the game if it is still raining.
5. If you pass the test you will get your driver's license.
6. You can do anything if you have your health.
7. If Chuck calls Fran, she will be very happy.
8. If you practice interpreting often, you will become more skilled.
9. Deaf people would have more access to our society if all TV programs were captioned.
10. The river will overflow if it rains one more day.

Congratulations!
You have completed Module Nine!

Module 10: Time Sequenced Ordering

Time Sequenced Ordering

10.1 Mini-Lecture
10 Minutes

Activity Goal   To comprehend the signed lecture and to identify the main characteristics involved in producing sentences using time sequenced ordering.

Activity Instructions

1. **VIEW** the mini-lecture provided by Nathie Marbury <u>without</u> sound or closed captions.

2. **SUMMARIZE** the mini-lecture in the space allotted below.

3. **CHECK** your understanding by **REPLAYING** the segment, this time with the sound/captions turned on (optional).

Mini-Lecture Summary

_____

_____

_____

_____

_____

_____

_____

_____

_____

_____

Module 10: Time Sequenced Ordering

10.2 Linguistic Information
10 Minutes

Activity Goal To provide the learner with a knowledge base that supports the learning experience.

Activity Instructions
1. **READ** the following information pertaining to time sequenced ordering.
2. **NOTE** any new information.

Linguistic Topic Time Sequenced Ordering

An ASL user will very often give information in the same order in which it actually occurred. In the examples below, notice how differently English and ASL treat the ordering of events...

Example 1
English order: I just saw a terrible accident!

ASL order: ACCIDENT, TERRIBLE, SAW (me)

Note: It makes sense from the perspective of a visual language that the accident would have had to occur prior to the signer witnessing it.

Example 2
English order: I am coming home late because the boss gave us a big job after lunch.

ASL order: LUNCH , FINISH... BOSS (t), BIG JOB, GIVE-US...HOME (t), ARRIVE LATE

Example 3
English order: I am tired because I got up so early this morning!

ASL order: THIS MORNING, EARLY, GET-UP (me), NOW, TIRED

When constructing a signed sentence using ASL, consider following the same order of events as they did or would occur. This type of ordering is called "time sequenced ordering."

Instructional Guide
©1995 Sign Enhancers, Inc.

Module 10: Time Sequenced Ordering

10.3 Video Practice Activity

"Interpreting & Transliterating Skill Development"
30 Minutes

Activity Goal — To practice transliterating using PSE and practice interpreting using ASL while learning from the models presented on the videotape.

Activity Instructions

1. **BEGIN** videotaped segment that demonstrates time sequenced ordering in the sample sentences.

2. **VIEW** written sentence on the screen, **STOP TAPE** by hitting the pause button.

3. **PRACTICE** transliterating the sentence using PSE.

4. **PLAY VIDEO** and **VIEW** model. **COMPARE** PSE rendition to your transliteration.

5. **PLAY VIDEO** and **REREAD** written sentence. **HIT PAUSE** button.

6. **PRACTICE INTERPRETING** the sentence using ASL.

Learning Tip — *As you practice formulating your interpretation for each sentence, remember to apply time sequenced ordering as addressed in this section.*

7. **PLAY VIDEO** and **VIEW** model. **COMPARE** ASL rendition to your interpretation.

8. **REPEAT** steps 1-7 for each sentence, incorporating the skills you have learned from the models.

9. **REVIEW** the sentences once more to **COMPARE AND CONTRAST** the ASL and PSE renditions of the models for:

   • Word/sign order.
   • Non-manual grammatical features.
   • Vocabulary/sign choices.

Instructional Guide
©1995 Sign Enhancers, Inc.

Module 10: Time Sequenced Ordering

10.4 Instructional Activity

"It's About Time!"
5 Minutes

Activity Goal To determine the appropriate time sequenced order using ASL for the sample English sentences provided.

Activity Instructions
1. **READ** the following English sample sentences.
2. **DETERMINE** the time sequenced order that would be used when interpreting the sentence into ASL.
3. **INDICATE** the appropriate ASL sequence for the sentences provided by **WRITING** the number indicating the portion of the sentence which would be signed first with a one (1), signed second with a two (2), signed third with a number three (3).

Example

Consider the actual order of events.
The car accident happened after I ate breakfast.
2   The car accident happened
1   I ate breakfast

Activity Sentences

1. I'm tired because I've been working hard all day after getting up so early this morning.

    ___ I'm tired
    ___ I've been working hard all day
    ___ getting up so early this morning

2. The traffic was backed up because of the accident.

    ___ The traffic was backed up
    ___ an accident happened

3. I stretch before and after exercising.

    ___ I stretch before exercising
    ___ I stretch after exercising

4. I've attended the biennial meetings since 1975.

    ___ I've attended the biennial meetings
    ___ since 1975

Instructional Guide
©1995 Sign Enhancers, Inc.

Module 10: Time Sequenced Ordering

10.5 Module Review

"Time Sequenced Ordering"
30 Minutes

Activity Goal — To review the information provided within this module by producing each sample sentence using ASL and PSE.

Activity Instructions

1. **REVIEW** section 10.2 Linguistic Information of this module.
2. **REVIEW** the sample sentences from the video segment in this section.
3. **READ** each of the English sentences provided in the section below and **APPLY** what you have learned by **PRODUCING** each sentence first using PSE, then ASL.
4. **CHECK** your work by referring to the glosses provided in the following section.

Learning Tip — *It is recommended that you videotape your work. Compare your signed renditions to that of the models on the video.*

Activity Sentences

1. The car accident happened after I ate breakfast.
2. I'm tired because I've been working hard all day after getting up so early this morning.
3. The traffic was backed up because of the accident.
4. I stretch before and after exercising.
5. I've attended the biennial meetings since 1975.

Comparative Translations

1. *English Sentence:*   The car accident happened after I ate breakfast.
   PSE Gloss: CAR ACCIDENT HAPPEN AFTER ME EAT-MORNING
   ASL Gloss: ME EAT-MORNING FINISH, HAPPEN CAR ACCIDENT

Module 10: Time Sequenced Ordering

2. *English Sentence:* I'm tired because I've been working hard all day after getting up so early this morning.

   PSE Gloss: ME TIRED BECAUSE ME WORK HARD ALL-DAY EVER SINCE GET UP EARLY THIS MORNING

   ASL Gloss: ME VERY-TIRED, WHY (rh-q), THIS MORNING EARLY, ME GET UP, WORK+WORK+ WORK+WORK ALL-DAY

3. *English Sentence:* The traffic was backed up because of the accident.

   PSE Gloss: TRAFFIC BACKED UP (CL:Bent 5) BECAUSE CAR-ACCIDENT (lft)

   ASL Gloss: CAR ACCIDENT FINISH (lft), TRAFFIC-BACK-UP (CL:Bent 5), STUCK

4. *English Sentence:* I stretch before and after exercising.

   PSE Gloss: ME STRETCH+STRETCH BEFORE AND AFTER EXERCISE

   ASL Gloss: ME STRETCH+STRETCH FINISH, EXERCISE+ EXERCISE FINISH, AGAIN STRETCH+STRETCH

5. *English Sentence:* I've attended the biennial meetings since 1975.

   PSE Gloss: ME EVER-SINCE GO+GO+GO EVERY-TWO-YEARS MEETING EVER-SINCE 1975

   ASL Gloss: 1975 EVER-SINCE, EVERY-TWO-YEARS, MEETINGS (t) GO+GO+GO (lft)

Instructional Guide
©1995 Sign Enhancers, Inc.

Module 10: Time Sequenced Ordering

10.6 Skills Application

"Time Sequenced Ordering"
15 Minutes

Activity Goal To practice applying time sequenced ordering to new stimuli.

Activity Instructions
1. **PRACTICE** applying the information and skills you have learned in this module by **INTERPRETING** the following sentences using time sequenced ordering.

2. **PRACTICE** transliterating each sentence. **COMPARE** the grammatical structure and non-manual markers to your ASL interpretations.

Learning Tips
1. *You can record these sentences onto an audiotape to more closely simulate a voice-to-sign interpreting situation.*

2. *It is recommended that you videotape your work.*

Activity Sentences
1. You can eat dinner after you do your homework.
2. I must take my medicine every morning after breakfast.
3. I was driving slowly after I saw the police car.
4. Joe will come home after a weeks training session.
5. Lori had to buy a light for the phone after she bought the TTY.
6. Tomorrow I am bringing an umbrella since it rained today and yesterday.
7. John is tired from working all day, then driving six hours.
8. Before I can come home, I need to go to the grocery store and the dry cleaners.
9. In order to be interviewed, you must submit your application and three letters of reference.
10. I can call you as soon as the meeting is over and everyone has left.

Congratulations!
You have completed all ten modules!
You are now ready to take the course assessment.

COURSE 2001 Assessment

ASSESSMENT: WRITTEN PORTION

"What Do You Know Now?"
30 Minutes

Activity Goal — To identify the learner's post-course knowledge pertaining to content addressed in this course.

Activity Instructions
1. **READ** and **ANSWER** all questions to the best of your ability.
2. If you are taking this course for credit, SUBMIT the completed test to your instructor or RID approved sponsor.

1. American Sign Language (ASL) is a language complete with grammatical syntax and cultural affiliation.
   a) True
   b) False

2. Pidgin Sign English (PSE) is a language complete with grammatical syntax and cultural affiliation.
   a) True
   b) False

3. PSE is also known as (circle one):
   a) "Contact Signing"
   b) "Continual Signing"
   c) "ASL/PSE Continuum"
   d) "Combination Signing"

4. Recently, linguists have discovered that regardless of the linguistic abilities of the communicators, PSE is comprised of ASL-based signs while maintaining English grammatical structure (primarily English word order).
   a) True
   b) False

Instructional Guide
©1995 Sign Enhancers, Inc.

5. The appropriate non-manual features that identify the topic of a sentence in ASL include which of the following (check all that apply):
   a) ___ Eyebrow raise to identify topic.
   b) ___ Eyebrow furrow (down) to identify topic.
   c) ___ Slight head tilt forward.
   d) ___ Signer leans back.
   e) ___ Last sign identifying topic is held longer.
   f) ___ Last sign identifying topic is dropped immediately.

6. The comment portion of a topic/comment structured sentence could be a (check all that apply):
   a) ___ Yes/no question
   b) ___ Wh-question
   c) ___ Statement
   d) ___ Command

7. For the following sentence, circle the topic of the sentence and underline the comment.
   Do you really want to go to that scary movie?

8. A wh-question is likely to include which of the following (check all that apply):
   a) ___ WHAT
   b) ___ HOW
   c) ___ WHO
   d) ___ WOULD
   e) ___ WHEN
   f) ___ HOW-MUCH
   g) ___ WHICHEVER

9. The appropriate non-manual features that identify a yes/no question in ASL include which of the following (check all that apply):
   a) ___ Eyebrows are raised.
   b) ___ Eyebrows are furrowed (down).
   c) ___ Head tilted slightly forward.
   d) ___ Signer leans back.
   e) ___ Last sign is held, waiting for a response.
   f) ___ Last sign identifying the question is dropped immediately so the response can be made.
   g) ___ Eye contact is made with the person being asked the question.
   h) ___ Drop eyes to indicate question is complete.

10. The non-manual grammatical markers associated with a wh-question include (check all that apply):
    a) ___ Eyebrows are raised.
    b) ___ Eyebrows are furrowed (down).
    c) ___ Head tilted slightly.
    d) ___ Eyes narrowed slightly.
    e) ___ Eyes opened wide.
    f) ___ Last sign is held, waiting for a response.
    g) ___ Last sign identifying the question is dropped immediately so the response can be made.
    h) ___ Eye contact is made with the person being asked the question.
    i) ___ Drop eyes to indicate question is complete.

11. Rhetorical questions are different than other kinds of questions because the person being "asked" the question expects the answer to be provided.
    a) True
    b) False

12. A rhetorical question's purpose is (check all that apply):
    a) ___ To show humor in communication.
    b) ___ To provide a linguistic mechanism for sarcasm.
    c) ___ To find out new information.
    d) ___ To introduce new information.
    e) ___ To show a causal relationship between two events.

13. Which of the following verbs would you consider to be directional verbs (check all that apply):
    a) ___ LOVE
    b) ___ GIVE
    c) ___ BORROW
    d) ___ SLEEP
    e) ___ SHOW
    f) ___ LOOK
    g) ___ TEACH
    h) ___ TYPE

14. Due to the spatial features of ASL, all verbs are directional.
    a) True
    b) False

15. The method of referencing a person or persons who are not present utilizes what we call "absent referents" or "indexing." When a signer establishes and uses a referent, the eyes usually (circle one):
    a) Maintain contact with the person being signed to.
    b) Will gaze in the direction of the referent.
    c) Will look at the index finger as it points to the referent.
    d) Will gaze down to indicate the referent is not present.

16. Some of the sign vocabulary that might indicate a negative include (check all that apply):
    a) ___ NOT
    b) ___ DON'T
    c) ___ NO
    d) ___ CAN'T
    e) ___ WON'T

17. Signs indicating negation are sometimes not even necessary if a negative headshake is simultaneously produced with the sentence.
    a) True
    b) False

18. Classifiers are a type of sign that represent a "class" of objects. They are used in ASL to describe the movement, placement, and visual characteristics of a person or object.
    a) True
    b) False

19. A classifier composed of the thumb, index, and middle finger (CL:3) can represent which of the following vehicles (check all that apply):
    a) ___ CAR
    b) ___ AIRPLANE
    c) ___ BUS
    d) ___ TRAIN
    e) ___ SKATEBOARD
    f) ___ TRUCK
    g) ___ BICYCLE

20. In ASL, when there is a relationship between two portions of a signed discourse, such that **if** one thing occurs, **then** something else will happen, the structure is called a (circle one):
    a) "Causal"
    b) "Circumstantial"
    c) "Conditional"
    d) "Conventional"

21. For the following sentence, identify the "IF" portion of the sentence by circling it and identify the "THEN" portion by underlining it:

    I'll teach you Sign Language in exchange for washing my car.

22. An ASL user will very often give information in the same order in which it actually occurred. In the example below, indicate the order in which each event would be signed by placing the number 1 (for first), 2 (for second) or 3 (for third) next to that portion of the sentence.

    I called the police immediately when I saw the burglar break into the house.

    a) ___ I called the police immediately
    b) ___ when I saw
    c) ___ the burglar break into the house

23. When the order of sentence components follows the actual order of events, this is called (circle one):
    a) Real-time Ordering
    b) Time Sequenced Ordering
    c) Reality Sequenced Ordering
    d) Conceptual Signing

24. The term "non-manual" refers to all physical expressions in Sign Language EXCEPT the signs themselves.
    a) True
    b) False

25. In the list below, label the linguistic features applicable to ASL with an "A," the features applicable to PSE with a "P," and the features applicable to both with a "B:"
    a) ___ Topic/Comment Structure
    b) ___ Rhetorical Question Format
    c) ___ Classifiers
    d) ___ Negation
    e) ___ English Structure
    f) ___ Time Sequenced Ordering
    g) ___ English Mouthing
    h) ___ Use of Space
    i) ___ Non-manual Markers

Congratulations!
You have completed
the Written Assessment!

Course 2001: Assessment

Assessment: Performance Portion

"What Can You Do Now?"
30 Minutes

Activity Goal To identify the learner's post-course skill level.

Activity Instructions
1. **RECORD** assessment sentences onto an audiotape to more closely simulate the interpreting task.
2. **PREPARE** room by setting up videotape camera and **VIDEOTAPE** your performance.
3. **TRANSLITERATE** each of the sentences using PSE.
4. **INTERPRET** (sign using ASL) each sentence presented below, incorporating the grammatical feature listed beside each sentence.
5. If you are taking this course for credit, **SUBMIT** your assessment videotape to your instructor or RID sponsor.

Learning Tip *Remember, if you are taking this course for CMP credit, you must submit the following to your sponsor:*

1. *Written Assessment*
2. *Performance Assessment Video*
3. *Course Evaluation (obtained from your sponsor)*

You may now turn the page to begin the Performance Assessment.

Good luck!

Performance Portion Sentences	Grammatical Features to Apply When Using ASL
1. It is important to eat breakfast every morning!	Topic/Comment
2. Are you addicted to watching TV?	Yes/No Question
3. How much did you pay for your car?	Wh-Question
4. I was just hired because I have 15 years of work experience.	Rh-Question
5. I need help because my car broke down.	Directionality
6. Who is that red-headed girl?	Use of Space
7. I can't find my glasses!	Negation
8. The man walked as if he were drunk.	Classifier
9. My boss will fire me if I call in sick again.	Conditional
10. I'm tired because I've been working hard all day after getting up so early this morning.	Time Sequenced Ordering
11. Are your interpreting skills improving?	Topic/Comment
12. Do you own your own home?	Yes/No Question
13. Did you want a hamburger or a salad?	Wh-Question
14. Dr. Johnson will be our speaker today.	Rh-Question
15. If you send me the letter I will give it to Tom.	Directionality
16. Sally wanted to go to the museum, but Joe only wanted to go to the restaurant.	Use of Space
17. I doubt if it will rain today.	Negation
18. The horse was running fast when all of a sudden he stopped dead in his tracks!	Classifier
19. Passing this course would make me very happy.	Conditional
20. I have been interpreting ever since I quit my counseling job ten years ago.	Time Sequenced Ordering

Congratulations!
You have completed Course 2001!

COURSE 2001 Appendix

Answer Keys

Getting Started Pretest:
Written Portion A.2 &
Assessment:
Written Portion

1. a
2. b
3. a
4. b
5. a, c & e
6. a, b, c & d
7. that scary movie (topic) Do you really want to go (comment)
8. a, b, c, e & f
9. a, c, e & g
10. b, c, d, f & h
11. a
12. d & e
13. b, c, e, f & g
14. b
15. b
16. ALL
17. a
18. a
19. a, c, d, f & g
20. c
21. washing my car ("if" clause) I'll teach you Sign Language ("then" clause)
22. 3, 2, 1
23. b
24. a
25. a) A b) A c) B
    d) B e) P f) A
    g) P h) B i) B

Module 1:
1.3 Topic/Comment Instructional Activity

"What's it all about?"

1. (My daughter) is smart. .... Same
2. Where is (my telephone book?) .... Different
3. It is important to eat (breakfast every morning.) Different
4. What is (your phone number?) .... Different
5. Can you postpone (my appointment?) .... Different
6. (That man) is famous because he used to be US president. .... Different
7. My favorite thing to do is (shopping.) .... Different
8. I like working on the (farm.) .... Different
9. Who is (your divorce lawyer?) .... Different
10. I really like (your picture.) .... Different
11. I want (lunch) now. .... Different

Module 2:
2.3 Yes/No Question Instructional Activity

"Yes or no, that is the question format!"
1. b 2. a 3. c 4. b 5. a 6. c

2.5 Yes/No Question Instructional Activity

"Are you raising your brows at me?"
The non-manual markers indicating yes/no questions are all the SAME.

Instructional Guide
©1995 Sign Enhancers, Inc.

Module 3:
3.3 WH-Questions Instructional Activity

"What do you know about wh-questions?"
1. who, what, when, where, why, how, which, how-much, etc.
2. end
3. beginning
4. ALL
5. ALL

Module 4:
4.4 Rhetorical Question Instructional Activity

"You skill, how (rh-q), practice!"
1. Me pass out **why?** going to the dentist.
2. The baby cried **when?** the dog barked.
3. I left quickly **why?** many people were angry.
4. The students were absent **why?** the flu.
5. Her father nervous **why?** all the noise.

Module 5:
5.3 Directionality Instructional Activity

"Which way did it go?"
1. give
2. help
3. to go to
4. borrow
5. borrow
6. asked a question
7. go to
8. helping
9. give me

Module 6:
6.4 Use of Space Instructional Activity

"Venturing into Space!"
Use of space features are used in ALL of the PSE and ASL sentences.

Module 8:
8.3 Classifier Instructional Activity

"In a class of their own!"
1. The <u>horse ran very fast!</u>
2. The <u>students lined up</u> at the door.
3. The <u>students sat in a semicircle with the teacher in the middle.</u>
4. The <u>man sat near the tree.</u>
5. The <u>cows</u> were all grazing <u>in the field.</u>
6. The <u>boy gets to school on a horse.</u>
7. The <u>car drove right into the house.</u>

Module 8:
8.5 Classifier Instructional Activity

"Have you seen any good classifiers lately?"
Classifiers are used in ALL of the ASL sentences.
Classifiers are used in numbers 2, 3, 6 & 7 in the PSE sentences.

Module 9:
9.3 Conditionals Instructional Activity

"If only..."
1. <u>My mom will be proud</u> (if I get an "A" on that test.)
2. <u>I will be broke</u> (if I buy that shirt.)
3. <u>The chair may break</u> (if you sit on it.)
4. <u>My boss will fire me</u> (if I call in sick again.)
5. <u>That little boy will cry</u> (if you don't give him a bottle.)

Module 10:
10.4 Time Sequence Ordering Instructional Activity

"It's about time!"
1. 3, 2, 1
2. 2, 1
3. 1, 2
4. 2, 1

Additional Skill Development Resources from Sign Enhancers, Inc.

Voice-to-Sign Interpreting Practice Tapes with Models
The following videotapes provide excellent voice-to-sign practice
with various model interpreters demonstrating their work.

6B	ASL Sentences (w/Guidebook)	ASL voc/ voice-to-sign demonstrations	20 min.
6C	More ASL Sentences (w/Guidebook)	ASL voc/ voice-to-sign demonstrations	45 min.
INT-LF	Interpretation Practice/Modeling	Three famous interpreting models	60 min.
TR-LF	Transliteration Practice/Modeling	Same models transliterate	60 min.

Educational Interpreting Practice Materials with Models
These videotapes provide actual lectures from the educational setting
with model educational interpreters demonstrating their work.

INT-EL	Interpreting Practice: Elem. Ed.	Interpretation Practice w/3 Models	40 min.
TR-EL	Transliterating Practice: Elem. Ed.	Transliteration Practice w/3 Models	40 min.
INT-HS	Interpreting Practice: H.S.	Interpretation Practice w/3 Models	40 min.
TR-HS	Transliterating Practice: H.S.	Transliteration Practice w/3 Models	40 min.

One-to-one Interviews: Interactive Practice
These tapes provide a unique interactive practice opportunity
with model interpreters; Sharon Neumann Solow and Rico Peterson.

7C	Interview: Apt. Manager & Tenant	Interactive interview with 2 model interpreters	60 min.
7D	Interview: Employment	Interactive interview with 2 model interpreters	60 min.

ASL Practice Series
This series of tapes enhances ASL skills
beginning with sentences and progressing to more complex material.

6D	ASL Practice Series: Sentences	Receptive & sign-to-voice practice with models	30 min.
6E	ASL Practice Series: Mini-stories	Receptive & sign-to-voice practice with models	40 min.
6F	ASL Practice Series: Stories	Receptive & sign-to-voice practice with models	35 min.
6G	ASL Practice Series: Dialogues	Receptive & sign-to-voice practice with models	30 min.
6H	ASL Funny Bones	ASL jokes: sign-to-voice practice with models	30 min.

Deaf Culture Lecture Series
This new series starts with a lecture on the cultural differences between Deaf and hearing cultures.

8I	Cultural Differences: Nathie Marbury	Sign-to-voice practice with model	35 min.

Instructional Guide
©1995 Sign Enhancers, Inc.

Course 2001: Appendix

Deaf Children Linguistic Samples with Models
The following tapes provide signed language samples by a variety of Deaf children with model voice interpreters demonstrating their work.

5A	Ten Year Old Signer: Stories with 2 models	Receptive & sign-to-voice practice	60 min.
5B	23 Samples of Deaf Children: Ages 9-19	Receptive & sign-to-voice practice	60 min.
5C	More Deaf Children Signers! Ages 5-11	Receptive & sign-to-voice practice	30 min.
5D	Even More Deaf Children Signers! Ages 11-14	Receptive & sign-to-voice practice	35 min.
5E	Still More Deaf Children Signers! Ages 13-18	Receptive & sign-to-voice practice	40 min.

Legacy of Learning Series
This new series starts off with two personal interviews between Sharon Neumann Solow and Lou Fant. Lou and Sharon conduct the interview in sign, then provide model voiced interpretations!

Leg-1	Legacy of Learning: Lou Fant	Sign-to-voice practice with models	60 min.
Leg-2	Legacy of Learning: Sharon Neumann Solow	Sign-to-voice practice with models	60 min.

Deaf Culture Autobiographies
These video resources provide sign to voice practice with inspirational stories regarding Deaf Culture.

8A	Gilbert Eastman/Int: Lou Fant	Receptive & sign-to-voice practice	40 min.
8B	M.J. Bienvenu/Int: Jan Humphrey	Receptive & sign-to-voice practice	40 min.
8C	Alfred Sonnenstrahl/Int: Lou Fant	Receptive & sign-to-voice practice	40 min.
8D	Paul Johnston/Int: Lou Fant	Receptive & sign-to-voice practice	30 min.
8E	Rev. Thomas K. Coughlin/Int: Kent Olney	Receptive & sign-to-voice practice	30 min.
8F	Dennis Schemenauer/Int: Lou Fant	Receptive & sign-to-voice practice	30 min.
8G	Patrick Graybill/Int: Lou Fant	Receptive & sign-to-voice practice	30 min.
8H	Howie Seago/Int: Lou Fant	Receptive & sign-to-voice practice	40 min.

Help for Fingerspelling
The software and video described below provide support for improving fingerspelling ability.

SW-1	Fingerspelling & Numbers Software	Fingerspelling practice	Windows 3.1
FS-1	Fingerspelling Videotape & Booklet	Two hour fingerspelling workshop	120 min.

For more information and a FREE catalog:

Sign Enhancers, Inc.
1-800-767-4461 (v/tty)
1535 State St.
Salem, Oregon 97301

Outside U.S.: (503) 370-9721 (v/tty)
Fax: (503) 370-6457

Instructional Guide
©1995 Sign Enhancers, Inc.

A Valuable Resource for Interpreter Education and ASL Instruction...

THE BEGINNING ASL VIDEOCOURSE

This award-winning 15 tape series is an excellent resource for several audiences. In addition to its exceptional ASL instruction methods, this series offers a variety of effective skill building options for interpreters. Included within each of the 15 lessons are: ASL interactions, ASL lectures, cultural information, linguistic information and creative storytelling.

Instructional applications for interpreters...

1) Sign-To-Voice Interpreting Practice

- Billy Seago and the Bravo family present ASL used within the context of daily life events. These entertaining segments provide both beginners and advanced interpreters a chance to focus on aspects of sign-to-voice interpreting other than receptivity such as: matching affect, vocal inflection, word choice, public speaking skills, etc. The segments are great for both consecutive and simultaneous interpreting practice.

- Cultural and linguistic information is presented in ASL by Billy Seago within each lesson. These lectures provide challenging linguistic samples for sign-to-voice interpreting practice as well as containing a review of valuable information for every interpreter.

- A sixteenth tape entitled "The People Behind the Bravo Family" provides a full hour of ASL interviews with the Bravo Family cast conducted by Billy Seago. These interviews provide a variety of content, varied registers and varied age levels. Beginners and seasoned professionals alike can enhance their ability to produce clear and concise sign-to-voice interpretations which truly match the signed presentation.

2) Voice-To-Sign Interpreting Practice

- Each Videocourse lesson contains wonderful sign-to-voice modeling. To practice voice-to-sign interpreting, simply listen to the voiced interpretations and practice your skills. Then, watch Billy and compare your interpretations with his signed presentation.

- These materials and instructional methods can be used for consecutive or simultaneous interpretation practice.

Call 1-800-767-4461 (v/tty) for additional ways to benefit from this rich resource.

A Resource For Those Who Teach ASL...
The Beginning American Sign Language Curriculum

This Beginning ASL Curriculum provides all the lesson plans so you can focus on your students! Simply follow the step-by-step instructions presented in the Instructor's Guide.

The curriculum components include:

- **Instructor's Guide:**

    15 pre-planned lessons each including: objectives, pre-test, experiential activities, lesson focus activities, video learning activities, comprehension quizzes, homework assignments, post-tests and more! Designed as a companion to the award-winning, proven, and highly acclaimed Beginning ASL VideoCourse ("Bravo Family" tapes).

- **Student Workbook:**

    This workbook makes it easy for students to follow along and track their progress. All activities are explained with user-friendly instructions. The Student Workbook contains clear illustrations of all sign vocabulary.

- **Activities Video**

    This video contains all linguistic stimuli needed to perform the instructional activities. Uses a variety of Deaf signing models from children to adults.

- **Assessment Video**

    This valuable tape provides a mechanism for standardized testing for each lesson.

- **VideoCourse lessons**

    13 hours of proven ASL instruction with the Bravo Family and Billy Seago. Each VideoCourse lesson includes Introduction to Vocabulary, Bravo Family Interactions, Cultural Notes, Grammatical Notes and Practice Sessions. Each lesson focuses on a specific unit of vocabulary presented within contextual situations including:

Lesson 1:	Meet the Bravo Family! - Morning Routine Signs
Lesson 2:	Breakfast with the Bravos - Breakfast and Dining Signs
Lesson 3:	Where's the TV Remote? - Household Signs
Lesson 4:	Let's go food shopping! - Food Signs
Lesson 5:	Review & Practice session - Lessons 1-4
Lesson 6:	Read any Good Fingers Lately? - Colors and Fingerspelling
Lesson 7:	A School Daze - School-Related Signs
Lesson 8:	A School Daze...The Sequel - More School-Related Signs
Lesson 9:	Dollar Signs - Money and Banking Signs
Lesson 10:	Review & Practice Session - Lessons 6-9
Lesson 11:	Playing in the Park - Nature & Sports Signs
Lesson 12:	The Doctor is In! - Medical Signs
Lesson 13:	Business as UNusual - Work Related Signs
Lesson 14:	Let's Go Clothes Shopping! - Clothes Signs
Lesson 15:	Review & Practice Session - Lessons 11-14
Tape 16:	The People Behind the Bravo Family - Billy Interviews the Cast

Call **1-800-767-4461** (v/tty) or (503) 370-6457 (v/tty) for more information about this user-friendly, comprehensive *Beginning ASL Curriculum*.

Notes:
A Page For Your Thoughts...